First World War
and Army of Occupation
War Diary
France, Belgium and Germany

56 DIVISION
Headquarters, Branches and Services
General Staff
1 April 1917 - 30 April 1917

WO95/2933/3

Published by

The Naval & Military Press Ltd

Unit 10 Ridgewood Industrial Park,

Uckfield, East Sussex,

TN22 5QE England

Tel: +44 (0) 1825 749494

www.naval-military-press.com

www.nmarchive.com

This diary has been reprinted in facsimile from the original. Any imperfections are inevitably reproduced and the quality may fall short of modern type and cartographic standards.

© Crown Copyright
Images reproduced by permission of The National Archives, London, England, 2015.

Contents

Document type	Place/Title	Date From	Date To
Heading	War Diary of "G" Branch 56th Division from 1st April 1917 to 30th April 1917 Volume XV		
War Diary	Beaumetz-Les-Loges	01/04/1917	08/04/1917
War Diary	Agny.	09/04/1917	19/04/1917
War Diary	Couin	20/04/1917	25/04/1917
War Diary	Hauteville	26/04/1917	26/04/1917
War Diary	Warlus	27/04/1917	30/04/1917
Miscellaneous	56th Division. G3/208	03/05/1917	03/05/1917
Heading	56th Division. Summary of Operations from 15th March to 19th April, 1917		
Miscellaneous	Summary of Operations 56th Division from 15th March to 19th April 1917	03/05/1917	03/05/1917
Miscellaneous	App I		
Miscellaneous	Instructions Regarding Burials of Soldiers.	07/04/1917	07/04/1917
Operation(al) Order(s)	56th Division Order No. 81	10/04/1917	10/04/1917
Operation(al) Order(s)	56th Division Order No. 79	04/04/1917	04/04/1917
Operation(al) Order(s)	56th Division Order No. 80	05/04/1917	05/04/1917
Map	Barrages for Brown Line		
Diagram etc	Map 'F' Areas For Reforming.		
Map	Neuville Vitasse		
Miscellaneous	A Form. Messages And Signals.	10/04/1917	10/04/1917
Miscellaneous	A Form. Messages And Signals.	13/04/1917	13/04/1917
Miscellaneous	A Form. Messages And Signals.		
Miscellaneous	A Form. Messages And Signals.	17/04/1917	17/04/1917
Miscellaneous	A Form. Messages And Signals.	11/04/1917	11/04/1917
Miscellaneous	A Form. Messages And Signals.	18/04/1917	18/04/1917
Operation(al) Order(s)	56th Division Order No. 84	18/04/1917	18/04/1917
Miscellaneous	A Form. Messages And Signals.	24/04/1917	24/04/1917
Operation(al) Order(s)	56th Division Order No. 86	26/04/1917	26/04/1917
Miscellaneous	March Table Issued With 56th Division Order No. 86		
Operation(al) Order(s)	56th Division Warning Order No. 87	29/04/1917	29/04/1917
Operation(al) Order(s)	56th Division Order No. 88	30/04/1917	30/04/1917
Miscellaneous	56th Divn. G.A. 234	07/04/1917	07/04/1917
Map	Barrages for Brown Line		
Miscellaneous	A Form. Messages And Signals.	09/04/1917	09/04/1917
Miscellaneous	A Form. Messages And Signals.	10/04/1917	10/04/1917
Miscellaneous	A Form. Messages And Signals.		
Miscellaneous	A Form. Messages And Signals.	10/04/1917	10/04/1917
Miscellaneous	A Form. Messages And Signals.		
Miscellaneous	A Form. Messages And Signals.	10/04/1917	10/04/1917
Miscellaneous	A Form. Messages And Signals.	11/04/1917	11/04/1917
Miscellaneous	A Form. Messages And Signals.		
Miscellaneous	A Form. Messages And Signals.	12/04/1917	12/04/1917
Miscellaneous	A Form. Messages And Signals.		
Miscellaneous	A Form. Messages And Signals.	13/04/1918	13/04/1918
Miscellaneous	A Form. Messages And Signals.		
Miscellaneous	A Form. Messages And Signals.	13/04/1917	13/04/1917
Miscellaneous	A Form. Messages And Signals.		
Miscellaneous	A Form. Messages And Signals.	14/04/1917	14/04/1917
Miscellaneous	A Form. Messages And Signals.	15/04/1917	15/04/1917

Type	Title	Date	Date
Miscellaneous	A Form. Messages And Signals.	16/04/1917	16/04/1917
Miscellaneous	A Form. Messages And Signals.	18/04/1917	18/04/1917
Heading	App. II		
Miscellaneous	56th Division Instructions Dress & Equipment.	01/04/1917	01/04/1917
Miscellaneous	56th Division Instruction. Tanks.	02/04/1917	02/04/1917
Map			
Miscellaneous	56th Division Instructions. Signal Communication.	04/04/1917	04/04/1917
Map	3rd Field Survey Coy. R.E.		
Diagram etc	1st Phase PB For Sending A For Receiving		
Miscellaneous	56th Division Instructions. Flags.	04/04/1917	04/04/1917
Miscellaneous	56th Division Instructions. Tanks (No.2).	04/04/1917	04/04/1917
Miscellaneous	56th Division Instructions. Contact Aeroplane Signalling Instructions.	04/04/1917	04/04/1917
Miscellaneous	56th Division Instructions. Concentration And Assembly.	04/04/1917	04/04/1917
Miscellaneous	56th Division Instructions. Signal Instructions No. 2 for Code Calls, Etc.	04/04/1917	04/04/1917
Miscellaneous	56th Divn. G.A. 124/1	04/04/1917	04/04/1917
Miscellaneous	56th Divn. G.A. 167	04/04/1917	04/04/1917
Miscellaneous	56th Division Instructions. Operations.	06/04/1917	06/04/1917
Miscellaneous	App VI		
Miscellaneous	Location Table.		
Miscellaneous	56th Divn. G.3/121	19/04/1917	19/04/1917
Miscellaneous	Casualties.		
Map	Heavy Artillery Barrage.		
Diagram etc	51B S.W. Ed. 4A		
Map	Situation 6 pm		
Map	Mercatel		
Map			
Miscellaneous	Neuv. V.H (2)		
Map	Situation 6 pm		
Map	Situation 6pm 11.4.17		
Map			
Map	Neuville Vitasse		
Miscellaneous	Glossary.		
Miscellaneous			
Map	Detail and Trenches Map b		
Map	Eterpigny. Map B		
Map	Map "A" France		
Miscellaneous	Glossary.		
Map	Neuville Vitasse		
Map	Map "A" France.		
Miscellaneous	Glossary.		
Miscellaneous			
Map	France.		
Miscellaneous	Glossary.		

(6202) W 11186/M1151 350,000 12/16 McA. & W., Ltd. (Est. 781) Forms/W 3091/3. Army Form W. 3091.

Cover for Documents.

Nature of Enclosures.

Vol/5

CONFIDENTIAL

War Diary
of
"G" Branch, 56th Division.
from 1st April 1917 to 30th April 1917
Volume

Notes, or Letters written.

WAR DIARY
or
INTELLIGENCE SUMMARY.

(Erase heading not required.)

Army Form C. 2118.

Place	Date	Hour	Summary of Events and Information	Remarks and references to Appendices
BEAUMETZ -LES-LOGES	1st April		Some hostile shelling of BEAURAINS and tracks in rear otherwise quiet. 51st Division Instructions "Dress and Equipment" issued. 167 and 168 Infy Bdes relieved 169 Bde in the line during the evening.	APPENDIX II APPENDIX III
"	2nd		No change. Considerable movement was seen behind the enemy lines today. One of our working parties digging an advanced trench was seen by the enemy and heavily fired on. 51st Divisional Instructions "Tanks" issued.	APPENDIX IV
"	3rd		Quiet day on the whole. Hostile artillery shelled the front line and BEAURAINS. 168 Bde carried out an intic battalion relief. Instructions from Corps received that zero day would be April 8th + that there would be a few days bombardment commencing 4th inst.	Appendix V
"	4th		Bombardment commenced. The enemy's retaliation has not been heavy. 51st Division Operation Order No 79 issued – Orders to Attack – The following Instructions were issued – Signal Communications – Flags – Tanks (No 2) – Contact Aeroplane Signalling Instructions – Concentration and Assembly – Signal Instructions No 2 for Code Calls etc. Also Orders re Signal Time + commencement of bombardment. Instructions received from VII Corps for Patrols to remain until dawn at first hours - Brigades informed.	Appendix VI

WAR DIARY
or
INTELLIGENCE SUMMARY.

(Erase heading not required.)

Army Form C. 2118.

Instructions regarding War Diaries and Intelligence Summaries are contained in F.S. Regs., Part II. and the Staff Manual respectively. Title pages will be prepared in manuscript.

Place	Date	Hour	Summary of Events and Information	Remarks and references to Appendices
BEAUMETZ - LES - LOGES	3rd April		W day: Our Artillery continued their wire cutting and bombardment. Wire reported cut in several places. This has not been confirmed by patrols. Enemy's artillery has not been active. Instructions received from VII Corps altering the "Brown" line objective. 51st Division Order No 80 issued accordingly. 167 Brigade carried out an internal relief.	APPENDIX I
"	"		Instructions received from VII Corps postponing Z day for 24 hours. X day. Wire cutting and bombardment continued, and good progress made. 51st Div. Instructions "Operations" issued. Zero hour received + issued.	APPENDIX II
"	4th		Q day. Progress made with wirecutting obstructive fire, and enemy reply was very slight. During the night, 1st LONDON regt. attempted to occupy NEUVILLE MILL, but were unsuccessful. Heavy artillery dealt with them during the day.	
"	"		At dusk, 1st LONDON regt. attacked NEUVILLE MILL but after obtaining a footing were driven out again with C.O.s of 5 officers and 50 O.R.s.	
"	5th	6pm	Y day. Wirecutting its concentration area took place during the night. Battalions continued a battle replies were slight except for heavy shelling of ACHICOURT. Div HQ opened in the railway embankment dugouts, AGNY.	

Army Form C. 2118.

WAR DIARY
or
INTELLIGENCE SUMMARY

(Erase heading not required.)

Instructions regarding War Diaries and Intelligence Summaries are contained in F. S. Regs., Part II. and the Staff Manual respectively. Title Pages will be prepared in manuscript.

Place	Date	Hour	Summary of Events and Information	Remarks and references to Appendices
AGNY.	April 9th.	a.m. 7.30	Zerohour. Assault commenced on VI Corps front.	
		7.45	Assault of 56 Div started	
		7.52	12th and 13th Londons reported through German front line with little opposition or casualties. Hostile artillery barrage slight. 14th Division on our left crossed crest of TELEGRAPH HILL and advancing in good order.	
		8. 0	3rd Londons reported in southern portion of NEUVILLE VITASSE.	
		8. 5	8th Middlesex and 12th Londons had been held up by uncut wire, but were now advancing. 3rd and 13th Londons progressing well through the Village. German barrage behind the infantry all the time.	
		8.10	168th Brigade reported assaulting troops had crossed PINE LANE and LEAF TRENCH on the whole Brigade front.	
		8-8.30	F.O.Os reports show that progress of infantry through NEUVILLE VITASSE is steadily progressing.	
		8.27	One Tank was approaching the Sugar Factory.	
		8.40	One Tank North and one South of NEUVILLE VITASSE going well.	
		8.55	168th Brigade message timed 8.12 a.m. reported 13th Londons on the BLUE LINE. 12th Londons had been held up by wire in front of PINE LANE, but were now approaching GRASS LANE TRENCH. 14th Division in touch with our left. Tank moving round the North of NEUVILLE VITASSE was on fire. Barrage in NO MAN'S LAND had stopped.	
		8.50	Batteries started to move to forward positions.	
		9. 6	Enemy shelling NEUVILLE VITASSE heavily.	
		9.20 to 9.50	Heavy hostile barrage in M.11.,17 and 24.	
		9.30	Div. M.G.Officer ordered to move forward.	

Army Form C. 2118.

WAR DIARY
or
INTELLIGENCE SUMMARY
(Erase heading not required.)

Instructions regarding War Diaries and Intelligence Summaries are contained in F. S. Regs., Part II. and the Staff Manual respectively. Title Pages will be prepared in manuscript.

Place	Date	Hour	Summary of Events and Information	Remarks and references to Appendices
	April 9th	a.m. 10.5	168th Brigade report right flank of 12th Londons in touch with 13th Londons in MOSS TRENCH, with left flank thrown back owing to right Brigade 14th Division being held up by wire about ACORN LANE.	
		10.0	167th Brigade report 3rd Londons in BLUE LINE, but 8th Middlesex held up by pocket of Germans at M.19.a.6.4.	
		10.10	C.R.A. reported leading Batteries had reached the forward position. Two tanks in action N.19.b.7.3. N.19.b.3.6. firing heavily due East. Hostile barrage now heavy on M.24 and between MERCATEL and NEUVILLE MILL.	
		10.20	168th Brigade report Reserve Coy. 13th Londons, was moving South through the Village to help the 8th Middlesex. 1 Coy. 12th Londons report themselves in the BLUE LINE.	
		10.30	Scouts of 13th and 14th Londons report wire between MOSS and TELEGRAPH HILL TRENCH passable and the latter weakly held. 14th Londons in assembly area ready to move.	
		10.45	Capture of BLUE LINE by 12th Londons confirmed.	
		10.55	167th Brigade report their Support and Reserve Battalions moving up according to programme. G.O.C. ordered 167th Brigade to extend the left of the 3rd Londons and join up with 13th Londons along the BLUE LINE using their Reserve Coy to do this.	
		11.20	167th Brigade report 3rd Londons on BLUE LINE and 1st Londons and 7th Middlesex pushing through towards second objective.	
		11.30	VII Corps asked to send a Contact 'plane to clear up the situation about N.19.a.6.4.	
		11.35	168th Brigade report 14th Londons had left their forward assembly area.	
		11.45	Situation at N.19.a.6.4. cleared up, and 8th Middlesex moved to the BLUE LINE - 68 prisoners and 4 Machine Guns captured here.	
		p.m. 12.15	30th Division on our right reported the BLUE LINE had been crossed under a heavy barrage	

Army Form C. 2118.

WAR DIARY
or
INTELLIGENCE SUMMARY
(Erase heading not required.)

Instructions regarding War Diaries and Intelligence Summaries are contained in F. S. Regs., Part II and the Staff Manual respectively. Title Pages will be prepared in manuscript.

Place	Date	Hour	Summary of Events and Information	Remarks and references to Appendices
	April 9th	p.m. 12.35	4th Londons placed at disposal of 167th Brigade.	Appendix I A
		12.45	9th Londons placed at disposal of 167th Brigade.	Appendix I B
		12.50	Wire received from VII Corps that time table must be strictly adhered to, and Brigades warned to carry this out leaving Supports at points that were holding out.	
		1.50	14th Division seen moving through N.15. Left flank of 30th Division had heavy losses from Machine Gun and shell fire, but were still advancing.	
		3.0	G.O.C. instructed 167th Brigade to form strong point at N.21.a.2.0 & defensive flank facing S.E. along LION LANE.	
		3.5	168th Brigade report that 14th Londons had taken the COJEUL SWITCH 1 Machine Gun and 100 prisoners.	
		3.10	Seven Guns of 193rd Machine Gun Coy. in position covering our left flank.	
		3.20	F.O.O. reports left of 30th Division held up outside its objective.	
		4.15	14th Division report themselves on the line N.9.c.50.25 - N.15.d.35.50 with their right in touch with 14th Londons, but no troops on the right of them.	
		4.20	G.O.C. ordered 167th Brigade to push forward 3 Coys. of 4th Londons to support of 7th Middlesex and work forward and get in touch with 14th Division N.21.b.	Appendix I C
		4.40	G.O.C. again told 167th Brigade to get in touch with 14th Division using the 4th Londons.	
		4.50	168th Brigade report that 14th Londons had gone right forward over their objective leaving only a few Platoons in the COJEUL SWITCH. 13th Londons being sent forward to clear up the situation.	
		5.20	167th Brigade report a pocket of Germans in IBEX TRENCH.	

Army Form C. 2118.

WAR DIARY
or
INTELLIGENCE SUMMARY
(Erase heading not required.)

Instructions regarding War Diaries and Intelligence Summaries are contained in F.S. Regs., Part II. and the Staff Manual respectively. Title Pages will be prepared in manuscript.

Place	Date	Hour	Summary of Events and Information	Remarks and references to Appendices
	April 9th	p.m. 5.30	168th Brigade ordered 13th London to occupy BACK and CARD Trenches, and 14th London to withdraw and reorganise, leaving out posts to cover consolidation.	
		5.35	F.O.O. reports Germans still holding out at M.20.b.0.3. and our troops digging in about N.20 central.	
		5.50	14th Division ordered bombardment of BROWN LINE to continue till 6.45 and then lift. G.O.C. agreed to prolong this barrage across our front and ordered 167th Brigade to move up 8th Middlesex in rear of 4th Londons ready to assist in this attack.	
		6.30	167th Brigade ordered 7th Middlesex to take IBEX TRENCH and push up LION LANE to night, and then to push out its left and gain touch with 4th Londons.	
		6.50	G.O.C. ordered 5th Londons to move up and replace 9th Londons if they moved.	
		7.30	14th Division report their attack on BROWN LINE had failed. Situation evening 9th April - see Situation map.	APPENDIX IV
		10.40	Prisoners passed through Prisoners' Cage during the day total 12 Officers, 72 N.C.Os. 538 O.R. from the 162nd, 163rd and 76th Infantry Regiments.	
	10th a.m. 12.15	---	Corps Order received. Assault on the WANCOURT LINE to take place at 8 a.m. VII Corps informed of the Situation of 56th Division and informed that assault at 8 a.m. not possible. The situation was not likely to be cleared up before daybreak.	Appendix V
		1.10	VII Corps informed 56th Division would be in a position to carry out assault about 12 noon.	
		1.30	VII Corps Order for the assault was amended and the assault is not now to take place until 14th and 56th Divisions report that the situation has been cleared up on their front.	
		2.20	O.O.No.81 issued detailing 167th Brigade with 9th Londons attached to carry out the assault on WANCOURT LINE.	APPENDIX I

Army Form C. 2118.

WAR DIARY
or
INTELLIGENCE SUMMARY
(Erase heading not required.)

Instructions regarding War Diaries and Intelligence Summaries are contained in F.S. Regs., Part II. and the Staff Manual respectively. Title Pages will be prepared in manuscript.

Place	Date	Hour	Summary of Events and Information	Remarks and references to Appendices
	10th	a.m. 7.45	During the night and early morning bombing parties of the 7th Middlesex and 1st Londons had made good the whole of the COJEUL SWITCH LINE as far South as LION LANE, but Germans were still holding out in the small system of trenches about N21.a.2.2. North of the SUNKEN ROAD. 14th Londons had established touch with 14th Division about N.15.d.5.8. and posts were being established along the WANCOURT LINE.	Appendix E
		9.16	One Battalion 169th Brigade placed at the disposal of 167th Brigade to replace 9th Londons who had been relieved from	Appendix F
		10.45	VII Corps Order extended the scope of the attack and ordered the troops after the capture of the BROWN LINE to continue their advance to the GREEN LINE, 56th Divn. occupying the high ground in N.21.d. and N.22.c. in support of 14th and 30th Division. Assault commenced at 12 o'clock.	
		p.m. 1.55	167th Brigade report that the advance was continuing with bombing parties down NEUVILLE VITASSE TRENCH and ZOO TRENCH. Left of 9th Londons held up by M.G.fire at junction of LION LANE and ZOO TRENCH. 8th Middlesex held up at cross roads N.20.b.7.5. by M.G.fire. 3rd Londons were late getting to position - T.Ms. being pushed forward to clear up the situation.	
		1.20	14th Division report they had captured BROWN LINE and wished to go forward to WANCOURT.	
		2.10	It is now clear that 14th Division had lost direction and their right flank is about N.16.c.9.1. leaving a large gap between their right and our left.	
		3.45	F.O.O. reports THE EGG now clear and our infantry advancing up the slope without opposition. In spite of a continued reports from all sources that the WANCOURT LINE had been captured, the situation in the evening as definitely ascertained is shewn on Situation Map. 14th Division advance on WANCOURT had been held up by M.G.fire from HILL 90.	Appendix G
		8.15	VII Corps ordered 56th Division to make good HILL 90 in order to assist the advance of the 14th Division.	Appendix H
		9.8	This task was allotted to 167th Infantry Brigade.	

Army Form C. 2118.

WAR DIARY
or
INTELLIGENCE SUMMARY
(Erase heading not required.)

Instructions regarding War Diaries and Intelligence Summaries are contained in F.S. Regs., Part II. and the Staff Manual respectively. Title Pages will be prepared in manuscript.

Place	Date	Hour	Summary of Events and Information	Remarks and references to Appendices
	10th	p.m. 11.52	VII Corps informed that it would be impossible for us to establish ourselves on HILL 90 during the night.	Appendix I
			Prisoners passed through Cage during the day 10 Officers 25 N.C.Os. 219 O.Rs.	
	11th	a.m. 12.45	167th Brigade ordered to capture NEPAL TRENCH between the COJEUL SWITCH and the 14th Division commencing 5.30 a.m. and to carry HILL 90 as soon as possible.	Appendix J
		8.0	167th Brigade report the junction of WANCOURT LINE with the COJEUL SWITCH was captured at 5 a.m. and counter attack beaten off.	
		8.40	8th Middlesex bombing parties making progress North and South from N.21.d.05.00.	
		8.45	169th Brigade warned to prepare to relieve 167th Brigade during the day.	
		9.10	NEPAL TRENCH between N.27.a.8.5.d N.27.b.1.9. was captured.	
		9.30	14th Division report that attack on WANCOURT was stopped at outset by M.G. fire from HILL 90.	
		10.15	1st London bombing parties commenced clearing trenches in N.27.b.	
		11.55	VII Corps O.O. ordering 56th Division to take the place of 30th Division and advance from HENINEL in touch with the 14th Division.	
		p.m. 12.30	One Tank is placed at our disposal for this.	
		1.0	8th Middlesex report they had joined up with the 1st Londons in NEPAL TRENCH.	
		1.30	167th Brigade reported post had been established at junction of HENINEL and USK Trenches.	
		4.30	9th Londons have posts established at N.28.c.05.40 & N.28.c.7.7. The HINDENBURG LINE clear of Germans as far as COJEUL River. 9th Londons also hold THE COT and C.T. towards HENINEL as far as N.28.a.2.6.	Appendix K

WAR DIARY
or
INTELLIGENCE SUMMARY

(Erase heading not required.)

Army Form C. 2118.

Place	Date	Hour	Summary of Events and Information	Remarks and references to Appendices
		4.30 a.m.	18th Manchesters of the Division on our Right, arrived at junction of COJEUL SWITCH and WANCOURT LINE preparatory to moving down COJEUL SWITCH LINE and attack trenches South of the River during the night.	Appendix IK
		4.47	169th Brigade warned to relieve 167th Brigade to-night.	Appendix IL
		9.15	Orders issued for 169th Brigade to consolidate HILL 90 to form a defensive flank towards WANCOURT and push patrols into HENINEL and when 30th Division have occupied HINDENBURG LINE to occupy the high ground in N.35.a. and 29.d.	APPENDIX IV
	12th	8.a.m. 12.50	For Situation see Situation Map. Prisoners captured during the day 7 N.C.O. 62 O.Rs. of the 86 & 31st Reserve I.R. Relief of 167th Brigade by 168th Brigade in Support Brigade Area complete.	
		7.0	Our attack started at 5.15 a.m. and enemy resistance was overcome and after stiff bombing 2nd and 5th Londons got connection in N.28.d. Enemy were then seen withdrawing from HENINEL in large numbers and leading Coy. 2nd Londons immediately pushed into the Village. High ground in N.22.d. was consolidated and strong points made. 30th Division on our right crossed the COJEUL RIVER and reached high ground along the COJEUL SWITCH.	
		9.40	2nd Londons established posts from N.29.a.8.4. N.29.b.1.8. and in touch with the 30th Divn. on its right N.29.c.5.4. HENINEL clear of the enemy.	
		10.30	Patrol of 2nd Londons occupied the Line N.29.d.2.0 29.d.8.9. where view of the country beyond was obtainable. Patrol also occupied the Line N.29.a.0.5. 29.a.4.9. joining up with 30th Division on our right.	Appendix M
		11.15	Patrol of 5th Londons entered WANCOURT and found it unoccupied, and posts were established at N.24.a.4.1.	
		11.55	14th Division report patrols in WANCOURT, and one Battalion moving North and one South of the Village trying to establish themselves on the GREEN LINE.	
		p.m. 1.0	VII Corps ordered the advance to be continued to the SENSEE RIVER	Appendix IN

Army Form C. 2118.

WAR DIARY
or
INTELLIGENCE SUMMARY

(Erase heading not required.)

Instructions regarding War Diaries and Intelligence Summaries are contained in F.S. Regs., Part II. and the Staff Manual respectively. Title Pages will be prepared in manuscript.

Place	Date	Hour	Summary of Events and Information	Remarks and references to Appendices
	12th	p.m. 4.30	169th Brigade Headquarters ordered to move to the vicinity of HENINEL.	Appendix O
		5.10	VII Corps ordered the GREEN LINE to be consolidated and Strong Reconnaissances sent forward towards SENSEE River.	Appendix P APPENDIX IV
		6.30	56th Division ordered to make all preparations to advance from the GREEN LINE the next morning For situation see SITUATION MAP.	
	13th	a.m. 12.5	Prisoners of the 86 and 84 Reserve I.R. were taken during the day.	
			VII Corps O.O. received ordering 56th Division to move forward on CHERISY, keeping in touch with the Division on either flank and taking advantage of their progress on the high ground.	Appendix Q
		12.50 p.m. 1.0	169th Brigade ordered to carry this out, forming defensive flanks where necessary.	
			Situation. Crest of the ridge from N.35.b.0.6. to within 20 yards of WANCOURT TOWER consolidated. 2 Battalions entrenches in depth with 6 M.Gs. The advance of the 50th Divn. has been held up by M.G.fire from West of GUEMAPPE, and now hold line N.24.c.5.3. N.18.c.3.0 The advance of the 30th Division along the COJEUL SWITCH Line failed to make ground.	
		5.45	Evening Report - Situation unchanged. Hostile M.G. fire from direction of GUEMAPPE and snipers, causing us some casualties. Shelling only occasionally and with light guns.	APPENDIX V
			Situation - see Situation Map.	
		6.30	VII Corps Order received for General Advance in conjunction with the VIth Corps. Zero hour at 5.30 a.m.	Appendix R
		6.40	169th Brigade warned that they would be required to carry out the attack and gain the line of the SENSEE RIVER.	
		10.10	O.O.No.82 ordering 169th Brigade to carry out the attack issued.	APPENDIX I
			Prisoners of the 84th, 86th and 99th R.I.R. were captured during the day.	

2449 Wt. W14957/M90 750,000 1/16 J.B.C. & A. Forms/C.2118/12.

Army Form C. 2118.

WAR DIARY
or
INTELLIGENCE SUMMARY

(Erase heading not required.)

Instructions regarding War Diaries and Intelligence Summaries are contained in F. S. Regs., Part II. and the Staff Manual respectively. Title Pages will be prepared in manuscript.

Place	Date	Hour	Summary of Events and Information	Remarks and references to Appendices
	14th	a.m. 6.50	169th Brigade reported the attack had started at 5.30 a.m. with approximately 500 yards gap between our left and 50th Division.	
		7.15	Enemy blew up WANCOURT TOWER during the night. Enemy barrage was quick in opening and heavy.	
			Enemy counter attacked our left flank strongly from spur in N.19.c. where the gap had been left driving back our front wave. Supporting waves pushed forward again but heavy enfilade fire prevented the attack making ground.	Appendix S
			169th Brigade wire timed 6.15 a.m. reported the attack appeared to go well over the Crest, and it subsequently appeared that a point O.31.c.2.7. was reached and a post established there, but it was withdrawn later as it was so far in the air.	
		8.0	169th Brigade report the attack on either flank had not made ground and the situation on the whole Corps front was as before Zero.	
		8.40	168th Brigade ordered to move 2 Battalions forward into the COJEUL SWITCH LINE North of the WANCOURT LINE.	
		9.5	169th Brigade report that as long as the Divisions on our right flank were unable to advance it was useless to try and push the attack on the Divisional front.	
		10.50	Situation on Divisional front was very involved. Portions of 3 Battalions 56th Division, 2 Battalions 50th Division being mixed up in N.30.a.	Appendix IV
		11.20	14th Londons placed at the disposal of 169th Brigade.	
		11.55	Division on our right reported strong German counter attack developing along the COJEUL SWITCH LINE. 169th Brigade ordered to be ready to take this attack in the flank should it develop and to secure Crest Line East of HENINEL strongly.	Appendix V
		p.m. 12.25	169th Brigade ordered 14th Londons to consolidate on HILL 90 as second line of resistance.	

Army Form C. 2118.

WAR DIARY
or
INTELLIGENCE SUMMARY

(Erase heading not required.)

Instructions regarding War Diaries and Intelligence Summaries are contained in F. S. Regs., Part II. and the Staff Manual respectively. Title Pages will be prepared in manuscript.

Place	Date	Hour	Summary of Events and Information	Remarks and references to Appendices
	14th	p.m. 12.30	VII Corps order that general advance should not be pressed owing to situation on the left.	Appendix V
		12.45	Division on our left reported enemy counter attacking and advancing against GUEMAPPE on a frontage of 1000 yards - strength estimated one. Brigade.	Appendix W
		1. 0	168th Brigade informed of this attack and ordered to occupy COJEUL SWITCH with a defensive line facing N.E.	
		1.40	F.O.O. reported enemy occupying trench in N.36.c. in strength and that our artillery fire had been observed to cause many casualties.	
		2.10	169th Brigade reported that the attacking waves are in shell holes 400 yards S.E. of the Sunken Road N.29.d.7.9. Officer of the 50th Division in charge.	
		2.15	168th Brigade warned to be in readiness to relieve 169th Brigade to-night.	
		3.30	168th Brigade ordered to relieve 169th Brigade during the night, and 167th Brigade to relieve 169th Brigade in Support Brigade Area during the next day.	Appendix IX
			Situation - See Situation Map.	Appendix W
		9. 0	VII Corps order leading Divisions to seize every opportunity of making ground on their front with the object of reaching the Line of the SENSEE RIVER by the night of April 16th	Appendix Y
	15th	a.m. 5.30	Relief of 169th Brigade by 168th Brigade complete.	
		p.m.	A quiet day was passed in consolidating the ground gained.	
		4.25	G.O.C. instructed 168th Brigade to establish themselves in the bombing trenches at N.30c. and d. during the night, and to join up their right flank with the 21st Division.	
	16th	a.m. 10.20	168th Brigade reported that 14th Londons had reached bombing trenches in N.30.c. and d. and found them about 2 feet. deep and full of water and had withdrawn.	Appendix Z

Army Form C. 2118.

WAR DIARY
or
INTELLIGENCE SUMMARY

(Erase heading not required.)

Instructions regarding War Diaries and Intelligence Summaries are contained in F. S. Regs., Part II. and the Staff Manual respectively. Title Pages will be prepared in manuscript.

Place	Date	Hour	Summary of Events and Information	Remarks and references to Appendices
	16th p.m.	6.55	Strong hostile barrage commenced creeping up the COJEUL VALLEY indicating a counter attack on GEUMAPPE against WANCOURT and possibly further South. 168th Brigade ordered to stand to on Hill 90.	Appendix I AA
		7.50	German counter attack did not materialize. 168th Brigade ordered to stand down.	
		8.15	VII Corps cancelled the order for advance to Line of the SENSEE RIVER, and said it would suffice if the leading Divisions could work forward to the Line T.6 central 0.31.c. 0.19 central in the next three days. Quiet day on the whole front.	
		8.30	168th Brigade reported heavy barrage on the whole front as well as on the front of the Division on our left and that they expected to be attacked. Support Brigade ordered to Stand to.	
		8.55	50th Division reported that Germans had recaptured WANCOURT TOWER and had also got into the Brigade on our right, but had been driven out again.	
		9.5	167th Brigade ordered to place 1 Battalion at the disposal of 168th Brigade on HILL 90.	
			50th Division attempted to retake the Tower during the night but failed.	
	17th a.m.	9.12	Arrangements made for the slopes East of WANCOURT TOWER to be swept by M.G. and artillery fire, while 50th Division counter attacked. 50th Division again attacked at midday and retook the TOWER.	
		5.10	Evening Report - considerable artillery and M.G. activity both sides of the COJEUL VALLEY, and HILL 90 heavily shelled.	
			O.O. No. 83 issued ordering 167th Brigade to relieve 168th Brigade in the line with 2 Battalions 169th Brigade at their disposal.	APPENDIX I
		7.10.	VII Corps Order for further advance received, such not to take place before 22nd.	
		7.35	This order was cancelled owing to receipt of preceding order.	

Army Form C. 2118.

WAR DIARY
or
INTELLIGENCE SUMMARY

(Erase heading not required.)

Instructions regarding War Diaries and Intelligence Summaries are contained in F. S. Regs, Part II. and the Staff Manual respectively. Title Pages will be prepared in manuscript.

Place	Date	Hour	Summary of Events and Information	Remarks and references to Appendices
AGNY	18th	9.35 a.m.	168th Brigade reported that the enemy were sending up our S.O.S. signal opposite our front.	Appendix BB
		11.0 p.m	50th Division report that information from a German prisoner points to hostile attack on WANCOURT TOWER about 1 p.m. All preparations were made for this eventuality.	Appendix I
		12.30	VII Corps Order for the relief of 56th Division by 30th Division by 20th Inst. received.	
		2.30	O.O. No 84 for relief issued. During the evening the relief of 167 Bde in the support was carried out. A guide was sent up to the POMMIER area. The remainder of the line was handed over and Div HQ opened at COUIN.	
	19th	3 pm am 12.30	168th Bde relief in the line complete. 167 Bde was relieved - the reserve area driving the day and marched to the SOUASTRE area dured.	
COUIN	20th		168th Bde proceeded to COUIN and Special in complete was slow were for all brances.	
	21st			
	22nd			
	23rd		Owing to attack of enemy 167 Bde gave rest to the HARLEY menin L battle. 169 Bde was assembled SOUASTRE	

WAR DIARY
or
INTELLIGENCE SUMMARY

(Erase heading not required.)

Army Form C. 2118.

Place	Date	Hour	Summary of Events and Information	Remarks and references to Appendices
COUIN	24th		Orders received from XVIII Corps that division would move up so as to be in position to go into VI or VIII Corps as required. O.O. No 85 issued.	APPENDIX I
	25th		1st & 1st Bdes moved by route march to GOUY en VIMEU & WANQUETIN during the afternoon. 164 Bde moved by bus to HABARCQ area.	
HAUTEVILLE	26th	3 pm	Div. H.Q. closed at COUIN and opened at HAUTEVILLE.	
		12.30am	Orders received for division to move to WARLUS area and to come under orders of VI Corps. Orders issued.	APPENDIX I
		2 pm	Div. H.Q. opened at WARLUS. Bdes moved by motor march in order attached	
		3 pm	G.O.C. and G.S.O.1 attended conference at VI Corps H.Q. and received orders to relieve 15 Division in the line.	
		6 pm	B.G.s.C. 163 & 164 Bdes attended conference at Div. H.Q.	
		8.45 pm	O.O. No. 86 issued with orders for relief in the line.	APPENDIX I
WARLUS	27th		164 Bde relieved 15 Div. reserve brigade by midnight.	

WAR DIARY
or
INTELLIGENCE SUMMARY
(Erase heading not required.)

Army Form C. 2118.

Place	Date	Hour	Summary of Events and Information	Remarks and references to Appendices
WARLUS	28th	9.30 pm	169 Bde relieved 167 Bde and this area became support area	
	29th	1 am	168 Bde moved its divisional reserve in ARRAS	
		10 am	Relief in the line by 167 Bde complete.	
		2.30 pm	Div HQ opened at Rue de la Paix, ARRAS.	
			O.O. No. 87 issued giving warning orders for a general attack on 3rd May and ordering	APPENDIX I
		3 pm	169 Bde to take over outer night action of the divisional front.	
			G.O.C. and GSO1 attended a Corps commanders conference at 12 Div HQ. ARRAS	
			Evening report - Quiet day.	
	30th	5 am	Relief of battalions of 167 Bde by 169 Bde in night action complete.	
			Morning report. Quiet night.	
		1 pm	O.O. No. 88 issued with orders for the attack on the 3rd May	APPENDIX I
		5 pm	Evening report - Quiet day.	

H.Q. 7TH CORPS.
G.C.R. **806**
Received **3.5.17**
Despatched

56th Division. G3/208

VIIth Corps.

      I forward herewith a Summary of the Operations carried out by 56th Division whilst in VIIth Corps.

C. Hull

H.Q. 56th Division.
2nd May 1917.

Major-General,
Commanding 56th Division.

File Reports by divs on operations

digging of assembly trenches in close proximity to enemy.

56th DIVISION.

SUMMARY of OPERATIONS from 15th March to 19th April, 1917.

As attack progressed opposition became more obstinate & did numbers and state of attackers render them more feeble?

SUMMARY OF OPERATIONS 56th DIVISION
from 15th March to 19th April 1917.

H.Q. 7TH CORPS.
G.C.R. 806
Received 3.5.17
Despatched

1. **PRELIMINARY PREPARATIONS.**

    On arrival in VIIth Corps Area the 169th Infantry Brigade took over the Centre Sector of the VIIth Corps front from 14th and 30th Divisions on the 14th March, the command being taken over by 56th Division on the following day.

    Preparations were at once commenced for the attack on the German Lines opposite.

2. **FIRST WITHDRAWAL OF ENEMY.**

    On the 17th March, however, information was received that the enemy had vacated his trenches, and that the 169th Infantry Brigade had at once pushed forward troops into BEAURAINS. This Brigade followed up the Germans until at nightfall we were holding the whole of his second line system along JACKMANN STELLUNG, MAIZIEU and MANCHE Trenches to M.18.c.4.8., with the left flank thrown back along the PREUSSEN WEG in touch with 14th Division which had occupied the German front line system.

    The enemy was holding the line TILLOY - THE HARP - TELEGRAPH HILL - NICE TR. - PINE LANE - NEUVILLE VITASSE VILLAGE and the trench of that name, together with the COJEUL SWITCH Line in rear.

3. **FURTHER PREPARATIONS FOR ATTACK.**

    Preparations were commenced for the attack on this line, and by the evening of 23rd March a forward trench had been dug running in continuation of DEODAR LANE through M.24. central to M.24.c.2.3. where it joined the advanced line held by 30th Division.

/On

On the 1/2nd April the 167th and 168th Infantry Brigades took over the Line from the 169th Infantry Brigade, the 167th Infantry Brigade being on the right.

On the 4th April 56th Division Order No. 79 was issued (Attack Order), and the preliminary bombardment commenced, wire cutting by Field Guns having commenced on 26th March.

On the 5th April the date of the attack was postponed until 9th instant, Zero hour being fixed for 5.30 a.m.; the attack, however, was being made in echelon from the left, the 14th Division actually starting at 7.30 a.m. and 56th Division at 7.45 a.m.

On the night 6/7th April and on the evening of the 7th, the 1st London Regiment attempted to capture NEUVILLE MILL, but were unsuccessful as it was strongly held by an advanced post of Germans with Machine Guns. As this post was liable to enfilade our advance, arrangements were made for a Tank to take this as its first objective on the day of the attack.

On the 8th April the final concentration took place, The German reply to our bombardment was not heavy except in ACHICOURT where several ammunition lorries were set on fire.

4. DISTRIBUTION OF TROOPS.

On the 9th April the troops were distributed as follows :-

On the right 167th Inf. Bde.

In front Line.- 3rd London Regt. on the Right.
8th Middlesex " " " Left.
1st London " in Support.
7th Middlesex In Reserve.
416th Fld.Coy.R.E. (less 2 Sectns)

/On

On the left 168th Inf. Bde.

  In front line.- 13th London Regt. on the Right.

       12th London Regt. " " Left.

       14th London Regt. in Support.

       4th London Regt. in Reserve.
        (less 1 Coy. Mippers Up.)

       2 Sections 193rd Div.M.G.Coy.

       512th Field Coy. R.E. (less 2 Sectns.)

       1 Coy. 1/5th Cheshire Regt. (Pioneers)

In Divisional Reserve. 169th Inf. Bde.

       8 Guns Div. M.G.Coy.

       1/5th Cheshire Regt. (less 1 Coy.)

       513th Field Coy. R.E.

       2 Sectns. 416th Field Coy. R.E.

       2 " 512th " " "

       181st Tunnelling Coy. R.E.

A map shewing the dividing line between Brigades, their Assembly Areas, and their respective objectives is attached (A).

5. METHOD OF ATTACK.

  The 167th Infantry Brigade was to capture the BLUE LINE with the 3rd London Regiment and 8th Middlesex Regiment. The 1st London Regiment was then to pass through and capture the COJEUL SWITCH LINE, and finally the 7th Middlesex Regiment was to go right through to capture the portion of the BROWN LINE (WANCOURT LINE) allotted to 56th Division. The 168th Infantry Brigade was to capture the BLUE LINE with the 13th and 12th London Regiments, and to send through the 14th London Regiment to capture the COJEUL SWITCH, the 4th London Regiment remaining in Brigade Reserve.

  As the success of the whole operation depended upon the success of the 14th Division on our left, the 168th Infantry Brigade was to be prepared to form a defensive

/flank

- 4 -

flank facing N.E. in case of non-success by that Division, and for this purpose had 8 Guns of the Divisional M.G. Coy. placed at its disposal.

6. THE ATTACK. Phase I.

The assault commenced at 7.45 a.m.

The 3rd London Regiment on the Right progressed well and at 10 a.m. it was reported that they had reached the BLUE LINE. This was confirmed at 11.20 a.m. The 8th Middlesex Regiment was at first held up by uncut wire and then by a 'pocket' of Germans in NEUVILLE VITASSE about N.19.a.6.4., but at 11.45 a.m. it was reported that this situation was cleared up and that the Battalion had reached the BLUE LINE having captured 68 prisoners and 4 M.Gs. in the 'pocket'.

The 13th London Regiment got through the German front line with little opposition, and at 10.5 a.m. were reported to be in MOSS TRENCH where they were in touch with the 12th London Regiment on their left. At 10.20 a.m. they were reported to be sending their Reserve Company South through the Village of NEUVILLE VITASSE to help the 8th Middlesex Regiment. The 12th London Regiment also got through the German front line easily, but were soon held up by uncut wire East of PINE LANE.

They continued to progress, however, and at 10.5 a.m. their right was reported to be in touch with the 13th London Regiment in MOSS TRENCH; their left was thrown back to keep touch with the Right Brigade of the 14th Division which had been held up by wire about ACORN LANE. At 10.45 a.m. it was confirmed that they had captured the BLUE LINE.

As regards the 4 Tanks allotted to co-operate with

/the

the Division, 2 to go round the North side of NEUVILLE VITASSE, and 2 to go round the South side, it appears that only 1 Tank crossed PINE LANE North of the Village and was subsequently set on fire. Of the 2 on the South side it was reported at 10.10 a.m. that both were still in action in N.19.b. These had done good work in helping to capture NEUVILLE MILL.

7. ACTION OF HOSTILE ARTILLERY.

The German barrage was late coming down and was reported at 8.5 a.m. to be well behind our Infantry. Between 9 and 10 a.m. it was heavy on NEUVILLE VITASSE and in squares M.11., 17 and 24.

8. ACTION OF OUR ARTILLERY.

At 8.50 a.m. batteries which had been previously detailed moved forward to positions as follows :-

281st F.A.Bde. & C/232 Bde. - in M.17.c., M.23.a. & M.16.d.
293rd F.A.Bde.   in M.23.b.(2 batteries) and
                            M.22.b. (1 battery)

At 10.10 a.m. these were reported to be in position.

9. THE ATTACK. - Phase II

The next phase, viz. the capture of the COJEUL SWITCH LINES by the 1st and 14th London Regiments and the advance to the BROWN LINE, commenced at 12.10 p.m. The 14th Division was to advance simultaneously on our left, the 30th Division on our right to follow in echelon.

Thus, whereas the 7th Middlesex Regiment (the Reserve Battalion of the 167th Infantry Brigade, which was destined to capture the BROWN LINE and pass through the 1st London Regiment after its capture of the COJEUL SWITCH) crossed the NEUVILLE VITASSE - ST.MARTIN SUR COJEUL Road at Zero plus 6 hours 36 mins. the 30th Division was timed to cross the

/NEUVILLE VITASSE -

NEUVILLE VITASSE - HENIN SUR COJEUL ROAD at Zero plus 6 hours 40 mins.

At 12.35 p.m. the 4th London Regiment (Reserve Battalion of 168th Infantry Brigade) was placed at the disposal of the General Officer Commanding 167th Infantry Brigade for the advance on the BROWN LINE, and at 12.45 p.m. the 9th London Regiment (169th Infantry Brigade) was also placed at his disposal.

In this phase of the attack the left got on, but the right was held up by strong opposition in the COJEUL SWITCH.

At 3.5 p.m. the 168th Infantry Brigade reported that the 14th London Regiment had taken the COJEUL SWITCH and captured 1 M.G. and 100 prisoners.

It was known that the 14th Division advance had progressed, and as reports from Artillery Observers shewed that the 30th Division attack had failed (held up by uncut wire) and that probably the 167th Infantry Brigade attack was held up for that reason, the General Officer Commanding 167th Infantry Brigade pushed forward the 4th London Regiment to support the 7th Middlesex Regiment and to gain touch with the 14th Division.

At 4.15 p.m. the 14th Division reported themselves as being on the line N.9.c.50.25 - N.15.d.3.5. and in touch with the 14th London Regiment, but that the latter had their right flank in the air.

The situation, therefore, appeared to be that on the left the 14th London Regiment had gone right beyond their objective leaving insufficient troops to mop up, while the 1st London Regiment and the 7th Middlesex Regiment on the right had made considerably less progress owing to the non success of the 30th Division, which left the enemy in LION LANE and about THE EGG free to turn their attention to our right flank, and also prevented us from pushing through to IBEX TRENCH which was still held up by the enemy.

/To

- 7 -

To clear up matters the 168th Infantry Brigade ordered the 13th London Regiment forward to occupy BACK and CARD Trenches, while the 14th London Regiment was to withdraw and reorganize.

167th Infantry Brigade ordered 7th Middlesex Regiment to take IBEX Trench and to push up LION LANE to the right at night, extending their left so as to gain touch with the 4th London Regiment.

Meanwhile 14th Division ordered the bombardment of the WANCOURT LINE to be continued with a view to an assault at 6.45 p.m., and at 5.50 p.m. the General Officer Commanding 167th Infantry Brigade ordered the 8th Middlesex Regiment to move up in rear of the 4th London Regiment ready to assist in this attack.

At 7.30 p.m. the 14th Division reported that their attack on the WANCOURT LINE had failed.

At 10.40 p.m. VII Corps Order was received for the assault on the WANCOURT LINE to take place at 8 a.m.

During the night the 50th Div. Artillery moved forward to positions in M.24.a., c., & d. and in M.29.c.

9. 10th APRIL.

The General Officer Commanding, at 12.15 a.m., telephoned the situation as then known, and pointed out that the 56th Division would not be in a position to attack at that hour, as the present situation was not likely to be clear by daybreak.

The VII Corps, therefore, amended the Order and arranged for the assault not to take place until the situation on the 14th and 56th Divisional fronts had been definitely cleared up.

At 2.20 a.m. 56th Division Order No. 81 was issued

/detailing

detailing the 167th Infantry Brigade with the 9th London
Regiment (169th Infantry Brigade) attached, to carry out
the assault on the WANCOURT LINE.

During the night and early morning the 167th Infantry
Brigade had made good the whole of the COJEUL SWITCH as
far South as LION LANE by bombing parties, but the Germans
still held out in a small portion about N.21.a.2.2. On
the left the 14th London Regiment had got touch with the
14th Division about N.15.d.5.8. and established posts along
WANCOURT LANE.

At 10.45 a.m. an Order from VII Corps extended the
scope of the attack and ordered the troops after capturing
the BROWN LINE to continue their advance to the GREEN LINE,
the 56th Division occupying the high ground in N.21.d. and
N.22.c.

The assault commenced at 12 noon. The 167th Infantry
Brigade made steady progress bombing down NEUVILLE VITASSE Tr.
and the COJEUL SWITCH, but the left of the attack on the
WANCOURT LINE was held up in the open.

The situation for the greater part of the day remained
very obscure, but by the evening it became clear that the
14th Division had established itself in the WANCOURT LINE
but had lost direction, and that their right flank was about
N.16.a.9.1. There was a large gap between their right and our
left, which was lying out in the open, while on the right
we had captured the whole of the SWITCH LINE as far as,
but exclusive of, its junction with the WANCOURT LINE.

At 8.15 p.m. VII Corps ordered the 56th Division to
make good HILL.90 1000 yards North-west of HENINEL, to
assist the 14th Division whose right had been held up by
M.G.fire from that HILL. This task was allotted to the
167th Infantry Brigade, but VII Corps was informed that it

/could

could not be completed that night.

The 167th Infantry Brigade was also ordered to clear the WANCOURT LINE between the COJEUL SWITCH and the right of the 14th Division.

During the night 281st F.A.Bde. moved to N.19.c. and 293rd F.A.Bde to N.26.a.

10. 11th APRIL.

During the day the 167th Infantry Brigade cleared up by bombing the whole of the COJEUL SWITCH and HINDENBURG LINE as far South as the COJEUL RIVER - also the WANCOURT LINE (NEPAL TRENCH) - THE COT (N.27.a.) and a new trench from that place towards HENINEL as far as N.28.a.2.6.

The 30th Division sent a Battalion to take over the portion of the HINDENBURG LINE captured by us, and to attack the trenches across the COJEUL RIVER.

At 4.47 p.m. the 169th Infantry Brigade was ordered to relieve the 167th Infantry Brigade, and at 9.15 p.m. it was ordered to make good the whole of HILL 90, and push patrols into HENINEL, and later, when the 30th Division had occupied the HINDENBURG LINE, to occupy the high ground in N.35.a. and N.29.d.

During the night 280th F.A.Bde. moved to N.19.c., A/281 and B/281 to N.33.a., 109th Battery to N.33.d. & D/281 to N.34.a.

11. 12th APRIL.

At 5.15 a.m. our attack started, and after stiff bombing the 2nd and 5th London Regiments working down the trenches on the N.E. and S. of HILL 90 got connection.

The enemy were seen withdrawing from the Village of HENINEL and the leading Company of the 2nd London Regiment

/immediately

immediately pushed into it. The 30th Division then crossed the COJEUL RIVER and progressed along the HINDENBURG LINE reaching the high ground; the 2nd London Regiment established posts from N.29.a.8.4. to N.29.b.1.8. and gained touch with the 30th Division at N.29.c.5.4., pushing forward patrols to N.29.d.2.0. - N.29.d. 8.9.

At 11.15 a.m. a patrol of the 5th London Regiment entered WANCOURT and finding it unoccupied established a post at N.24.a.4.1.

At 11.55 a.m. the 14th Division moved ~~to~~ a Battalion round each side of WANCOURT with a view to gaining the GREEN LINE.

At 1 p.m. VII Corps ordered the advance to be continued to the SENSEE River but at 5.10 p.m. these orders were modified, and the 56th Division was ordered to consolidate, to send forward strong reconnaissances and to make all preparations to advance on the 13th instant.

During the night 293rd F.A.Bde. moved to positions in N.33.c. and N.34.a. and 280th F.A.Bde. to positions along the road in N.27.c.

12. 13th APRIL.

At 12.5 a.m. VII Corps order was received to the effect that the 56th Division was to move forward on CHERISY, keeping in touch with the Divisions on either flank, and taking advantage of their progress on the high ground.

At 1 p.m. the situation was that the 50th Division on our left had been held up by M.G. fire from the W. of GUEMAPPE, while the 30th Division on our right had failed to make ground.

The 169th Infantry Brigade held the Crest of the ridge from N.35.b.0.6. to within 20 yards of WANCOURT TOWER.

The 50th Division were reported to be echelonned back

/from

from N.24.c.5.3. to N.18.c.3.0.

At 6.30 p.m. VII Corps Orders were received for a general advance on the 14th April, in conjunction with VI Corps, the objective being the Line of the SENSEE RIVER and

169th Infantry Brigade was detailed to carry out the attack.

13. 14th APRIL.

During the night the enemy blew up WANCOURT TOWER.

Our attack started at 5.30 a.m. but there was a gap of about 500 yards between our left and the 50th Division; it appears that the latter, starting from the line of the COJEUL RIVER, lost direction somewhat and came across our left rear. As soon as the attack started our left flank was strongly counter attacked from the SPUR in N.19.c. and the front wave pushed back. Supporting waves pushed forward again, but heavy enfilade fire and the fact that the creeping barrage had got ahead prevented the attack making ground.

Apparently a few troops reached a point about O.31.c.2.7. but as it was so much in the air they subsequently withdrew.

At 8 a.m. it was clear that the attacks by both flank Divisions had failed, and that the situation was as before the assault started.

Troops were very much mixed up, there being portions of 3 Battalions 56th Division and 2 Battalions 50th Division in N.30.a., and, as it was reported that a strong German counter-attack was developing towards the HINDENBURG LINE from the North-east, the 14th London ~~London~~ Regiment was placed under the orders of the 169th Infantry Brigade, and

/the

the latter ordered to be prepared to take this counter-attack in flank should it develop. No attack did, however, develop, and as the VII Corps ordered the attack not to be pressed further owing to the situation on the left, opportunity was taken to relieve the 169th Infantry Brigade by the 168th Infantry Brigade, the former going into Reserve, and the 167th Infantry Brigade moving up from Reserve to Support.

14. 15th - 16th APRIL.

The 15th was occupied in consolidating the ground.

On the 16th, the 14th London Regiment attempted to advance the line by occupying the German practice trenches in N.30.c. and d., but finding them only 2 ft. deep and full of water they withdrew.

A strong hostile barrage creeping up the COJEUL VALLEY about 7 p.m. made it appear that the Germans were going to attack, and measures were taken accordingly; but it subsequently appeared that the shelling was with a view to cover a German relief on our front.

However, at dusk the Germans bombarded heavily again and captured WANCOURT TOWER from the 50th Division.

15. 17th APRIL.

At midday on 17th April, the 50th Division attacked and recaptured the TOWER, our artillery and M.Gs. co-operating by sweeping the slope to the East.

The proposed relief of the 168th Infantry Brigade by the 167th Infantry Brigade was cancelled owing to the receipt of a Corps Order that there would be no further advance before the 22nd instant.

C/232 Bde. R.F.A. was withdrawn from action during the night.

/16.

16. 18th APRIL.

On the 18th April, the relief of the 56th Division by the 30th Division commenced and was complete on the night of the 20th, the command of the line being handed over at 3 p.m. on the 19th April.

17. PRISONERS CAPTURED.

The number of unwounded prisoners captured by the 56th Division during these operations was as follows :-

	Officers.	N.C.Os.	Men.
9th April	12	72	538.
10th "	10	25	219.
11th "	-	7	62.
12th "	-	1	12.
13th "	-	-	4.
14th "	-	-	3.
	22.	105.	838.

18. CASUALTIES.

Our casualties from 9th to 20th April inclusive were :-

	Officers.	O.Rs.
9th April	37	844.
10th ")		
11th ")		
12th ")	23	298.
13th ")		
14th "	24	705.
15th "	-	27
16th "	6	97.
17th "	1	22.
18th "	2	35.
19th "	1	11.
20th "	-	7.
	94.	2,046

App I

SECRET.

AQS 216.

INSTRUCTIONS REGARDING BURIALS OF SOLDIERS. (Continued).

RECOGNISED CEMETERIES:

(a) Whenever possible, bodies should be buried in one of the following cemeteries, which are marked "BRITISH MILITARY CEMETERY".

BEAURAINS ROAD CEMETERY.		M.4.b.5.5.	(51.b.)
ACHICOURT ROAD "	.	M.4.c.1.8.	(")
"A" "	.	M.16.b.8.8.	(")
"B" "	.	M.18.c.4.9.	(")
ACHICOURT CHURCHYARD CEMETERY.		G.33.c.3.6.	(")
AGNY "	.	M.2.b.9.3.	(")
WAILLY "	.	R.22.b.4.7.	(51.c.)

(b) None of the above Cemeteries are in charge of caretakers. It will therefore be the duty of the Officer i/c of the Burial party, or the Chaplain who superintends the Burial, to take action as regards "Registration of Graves" and "Disposal of Effects", as laid down in paras 2 and 3 of "Instructions regarding Burials" issued under this Office AQS 216 of 4th instant.

(c) If the Chaplain or other person superintending the burial is not in possession of the specially prepared A.B.136 he must transmit particulars of the burial to Captain HARTLEY, whose Headquarters will be at M.2.c.8.5. (300 yards north of AGNY CHATEAU).

for Lieut. Colonel,
A.A.& Q.M.G., 56th Division.

5.4.17.

SECRET. 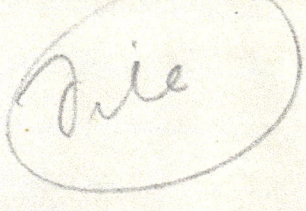 Copy No. 5

56th DIVISION ORDER NO. 81.

10
9th April, 1917.

1. On our left the VIth Corps is in possession of the WANCOURT - FEUCHY Line N. of FEUCHY CHAPELLE.

2. The 56th and 14th Divisions are to assault the WANCOURT - FEUCHY Line simultaneously with the 3rd Division today.

3. 56th Division Objective from N.27.a.9.5. to road junction at N.22.a.5.5. 14th Division Objective from above road to N.16.Central. 21st and 30th Divisions will support this attack with their Artillery but they will not move until the WANCOURT - FEUCHY Line is taken.

4. The 167th Infantry Brigade will carry out the attack on the front assigned to the 56th Division. The 9th Londons are placed at the disposal of the G.O.C., 167th Infantry Brigade.

5. Barrage Lines and times will be notified later.

6. Zero hour will be notified later.

7. The Operation will not take place until the situation on 56th and 14th Division fronts is cleared up; it is very important that 168th Infantry Brigade should get touch with the right of the 14th Division and clear any Enemy out of the NEUVILLE VITASSE - WANCOURT Road in 21.a.

8. ACKNOWLEDGE.

Hqrs., 56th Division.   L.A.Newnham
                          Captain for Lt.Colonel,
                          General Staff.

Addressed 167th Infantry Brigade
Repeated 168th   "   "   VIIth Corps H.A. *
          169th   "   "   14th Division *
          C.R.A.   30th Division *
          VIIth Corps *

* Telegraphic Summaries only sent to these formations.

Issued by Special D.R.
3.70 a.m.

SECRET.   Copy No ...31...

56th DIVISION ORDER No. 79

Reference attached Maps 1/20,000 .... (C)
& 1/5,000 NEUVILLE VITASSE .... (D)
Artillery Barrage Maps   .... (E1) (E2) (E3).
Areas for Reforming   .... (F)

                                                             4th April, 1917.

Line held by enemy. 1. The Line now held by the enemy is shewn in RED on Map "C". The front from THE HARP to the COJEUL RIVER is held by the 23rd (Reserve) Saxon Division.

General Objective of Corps. 2. In conjunction with an attack by the First Army, the Third Army is to break through the enemy's defences and advance on CAMBRAI.

The VII Corps is to attack on the right of and simultaneously with VI Corps.

The dividing lines between Divisions and their successive objectives are shown on the attached Map "C".

Objective of 56th Division. 3. The 56th Division will capture the hostile defences shown within the Divisional boundaries on the attached Map "C" and will then establish itself on the BROWN Line. The Boundary between Brigades is shown on the attached Map "C" and also in detail through NEUVILLE VITASSE Village on Map "D".

Method of Attack. 4. The attack of 56th Division will be carried out by 167th Infantry Brigade on the right and by 168th Brigade on the left up to and including the Easternmost trench of the HINDENBURG LINE (or COJEUL SWITCH) N.14.c.95.55. - N.21.c.30.95, from which line 167th Infantry Brigade will carry on the attack on to the BROWN LINE.

/167th

167th Infantry Brigade will keep a reserve in hand so that it may have troops available to assist the advance of the 30th Division by taking in flank and reverse trenches included in the objective of the latter.

5. The programme of attack will be as follows :—

    (a) The assault will be delivered on "Z" day.

    (b) The preparatory bombardment of the enemy's defences will be carried out on "V", "W", "X" and "Y" days.

    (c) <u>Programme on "Z" day</u>

<u>At Zero</u> — VI Corps to assault.

<u>At Zero plus 2 hours</u> — 14th Division will advance.

<u>At Zero plus 2 hours 15 mins.</u> — Barrage for 56th Divn. will be put down 50 yards short of the German front line as shown on the barrage map, and our Infantry will leave the trenches.

The barrage will be lifted after one minute on to the front line whence it will lift at varying times according as the Infantry arrive within assaulting distance. It will then begin to creep.

On reaching the BLUE LINE there will be a halt, after which 167th and 168th Infantry Brigades will assault the HINDENBURG LINE (COJEUL SWITCH) as below.

<u>At Zero plus 6 Hours 36 mins.</u> — The troops of the 167th Infantry Brigade detailed for the attack on the HINDENBURG (COJEUL SWITCH) LINE will cross the sunken road N.20.c.6.2.- N.20.a.1.6. and assault.

<u>At Zero plus 6 hours 40 minutes.</u> — The troops of 168th Infantry Brigade detailed for the attack on the same objective will assault

As soon as the Easternmost trench of the HINDENBURG LINE has been captured, the 56th Divisional Artillery will form a protective barrage on a North and South Line lasting for 30 minutes, under cover of which the troops of 167th Infantry Brigade detailed for the attack on the WANCOURT — FEUCHY Line will advance close to the barrage.

The barrage will then move forward at the rate of 100 yds. in 2 minutes, gradually swinging round until it is square with the objective.

- 3 -

<u>Limits of Advance.</u>	6.	The limit of advance of the 14th Division is the BROWN LINE.

Similarly the BROWN LINE is the limit of the advance of the 56th Division.

The 30th Division is to push through to the GREEN LINE, extending its left on leaving the BROWN LINE, so as to gain touch with VI Corps on the left.

<u>Defensive flank.</u>   7.   G.O.C. 168th Infantry Brigade will be prepared to form a defensive flank facing North-east in the event of the enemy's line on the North not being broken.

This defensive flank will follow generally the line N.14.c.0.2. - N.13.d.6.3. - N.13.b.1.0. - N.13.a.8.2. - N.13.a.6.2. - thence the Northern Boundary of the Division, and will consist of a series of strong points.

<u>Strong Points for the BLUE LINE.</u>   8.   As soon as the BLUE LINE has been captured, strong points will be at once constructed approximately at the following points :-

     167th Inf.Bde.   near the SUGAR FACTORY
                                         (N.19.d.)

                                 N.19.b.8.2.(junction of THE OVAL and NEUVILLE VITASSE Trench)

                                 N.20.a.55.40.
                                 N.20.a.35.00.
     168th Inf.Bde.   N.20.a.30.65 (S. end of MOSS TRENCH)

                                 N.14.c.0.2.
                                 N.13.d.6.3.
                                 N.13.b.1.0.

Strong Points in Advance of the BLUE LINE

9. As soon as the Easternmost trench of the HINDENBURG LINE (or COJEUL SWITCH) has been captured by 167th and 168th Infantry Brigade, and during the advance of the troops of the former to the BROWN LINE, consolidation or the digging of a new trench will be immediately commenced and Strong Points constructed as necessary. Similarly the BROWN LINE will be consolidated when captured.

Reforming.

10. As soon as WANCOURT has been captured by 30th Division, troops of 56th Division will be reformed in the areas shown in Map "F", covered by outposts of the 167th Infantry Brigade on the BROWN LINE.

Assembly Areas.

11. Assembly Areas of Brigades have been circulated under 56th Division Instructions "Assembly Areas"

All troops will be in their final battle positions by 3 a.m. on the night Y/Z.

Artillery Barrages & Time Table.

12. Map of Artillery Barrages is attached (D).

The rate of the creeping barrage is calculated at 100 yards in 4 minutes, except where the nature of the objective is likely to retard progress, when it is calculated at 100 yards in 6 minutes.

Artillery.

13. Command (a). All the Artillery attached to 56th Division is placed under the orders of the G.O.C. R.A. VII Corps, who will deal direct with C.R.A. 56th Division.

It will so remain until the capture of the BLUE Line when it will come under the orders of the G.O.C. 56th Division.

Heavy Artillery (b) 56th Division will have a call on "E" Group (85th Heavy Artillery Group) composed of 12 60-pdrs - 24 6" Hows. and 8 8" Howitzers -

H. Qrs.

H. Qrs. AGNY. One Officer of the Heavy Artillery will be attached to each Infantry Brigade for liaison purposes.

Moves of Artillery (c) On the capture of the BLUE LINE Artillery of the 56th Division will move forward under the orders of the C.R.A. to positions as under :-

  281st Bde. (& C/232) - M.17.c.6.2. - M.23.a.35.65.
  293rd Bde. (2 Batteries) M.23.b.60.45 - M.23.b.55.85.
   "   (1 Battery) - M.22.b.80.60 -
  D/281st Bde.   - M.16.d.80.80.

Use of Gas. 14. Gas Projectors will not be used.

Allotment of R.E. & Pioneers. 15. The allotment of R.E. and Pioneers for the purpose of consolidation and constructing Strong Points after the attack has succeeded has already been issued in 56th Division Instructions "Employment of R.E. & Pioneers"

Contact Aeroplanes. 16. Contact aeroplanes will call by Klaxon horn for flares to be lit by the leading troops as near as possible at the following hours :-

  Zero plus 3 hours 30 minutes.
  Zero plus 7 hours 30 minutes.
  Zero plus 8 hours 30 minutes.
  Zero plus 11 hours.

  Further details are being given under 56th Div. Instructions "Contact Aeroplanes".

  When the aeroplane calls for flares a few only will be lit each time under the orders of Platoon Commanders.

Machine Guns. 17. Orders for the co-operation of Machine Guns have been issued under 56th Division Instructions "Action of Massed Machine Guns".

/18.

Action of Tanks.	18.	One Section (4) Tanks have been allotted to co-operate with the 56th Division.

These will start close behind the leading wave of Infantry.

One half Section (2) Tanks will be directed round the North side of the Village of NEUVILLE VITASSE, with the special mission of attacking the Strong Point N.19.b.65.90.

The other half Section will be directed round the Southern edge of the North-eastern portion of that Village, with the special mission of attacking the Strong Point N.20.a.4.4.

Further details are contained in 56th Division Instructions "Tanks". |
| Synchronization of Watches. | 19. | From W day (inclusive) O.C. Divisional Signals will send round a Despatch Rider with a Watch to give correct time to G.O's C. all Infantry Brigades and to the C.R.A. between the hours of 10 a.m. and 12 noon daily.

On Y day the Despatch Rider will also visit the above between 4 p.m. and 6 p.m.

Signal time will also be given as usual up to "Y" day (inclusive) by telephone at 9 a.m. |
| Medical. | 20. | Medical arrangements have been issued under 56th Division Instructions "Medical Arrangements" |
| Z day and Zero Hour. | 21. | Z day will be 8th April.

Zero hour will be communicated later. |
| Advanced Div. H. Qrs. | 22. | Advanced Divisional Headquarters will be established in the dugouts under the Railway Embankment at M.3.c.5.1. at 6 p.m. on the evening of Y day. |

Head Qrs. 56th Divn.
4th April, 1917.

Lieut-Colonel,
General Staff.

56th Div. Order No. 79.

Copies to -

1. 167th Infantry Brigade.
2. 168th Infantry Brigade.
3. 169th Infantry Brigade.
4. VII Corps.
5. "   "   Artillery.
6. "   "   Heavy Artillery.
7. "   "   M.G.Officer.
8. 14th Division.
9. 30th Division.
10. C.R.A.
11. C.R.E.
12. 1/5th Cheshire Regt.
13. A.P.M.
14. 193rd Div.M.G.Coy.
15. 56th Div. Signals.
16. 1st Bde. H.B. M.G.Corps.
17. "D" Bn.   "   "   "
18. Lieut.BELL, c/o "D" Bn.
19. 56th Div. Train.
20. Div. M.G.Officer.
21. Div. Gas Officer.
22. D.A.D.....
23. 4th Aust. Div.Sup.Col.
24. No.2 Ammn.Sub Park.
25. A.D.V.S.
26. No.8 Squadron R.F.C.
27. G.O.C.
28. A.D.C.
29. A.D.M.S.
30. "Q"
31. War Diary.
32. File.

Map E3 will be issued later.

SECRET.　　　　　　　　　　　　　　　　　　　　　　Copy No.....

War Diary

31

56th DIVISION ORDER No. 80.

5th April 1917.

1. With reference to 56th Division Order No. 79 of 4.4.17, para. 6, the second objective of 30th and 56th Divisions will be NEPAL TRENCH.

2. The BROWN LINE on Maps C & E2 will, therefore, be brought back along that trench from N.18.d.00. to N.27.a.84. thence Southwards through ST.MARTIN-SUR-COJEUL to join BLUE and BLACK Line.

The dividing line between Divisions and position of the GREEN LINE remain unaltered.

3. ACKNOWLEDGE.

B Pakenham

Head Qrs. 56th Divn.　　　　　　　　　　　Lieut-Colonel,
　　　　　　　　　　　　　　　　　　　　　　General Staff.

Issued at 2 pm

Copies to -

1. 167th Infantry Brigade.
2. 168th Infantry Brigade.
3. 169th Infantry Brigade.
4. VII Corps.
5. " " Artillery.
6. " " Heavy Artillery.
7. " " M.G.Officer.
8. 14th Division.
9. 30th Division.
10. C.R.A.
11. C.R.E.
12. 1/5th Cheshire Regt.
13. A.P.M.
14. 193rd Div.M.G.Coy.
15. 56th Div. Signals.
16. 1st Bde. H.B.M.G.Corps.
17. "D" Bn. " " "
18. Lieut.BELL, c/o "D" Bn.
19. 56th Div. Train.
20. Div. M.G.Officer.
21. Div. Gas Officer.
22. D.A.D.O.S.
23. 4th Aust.Div.Sup.Col.
24. No.2 Ammn.Sub Park.
25. A.D.V.S.
26. No.8 Squadron R.F.C.
27. G.O.C.
28. A.D.C.
29. A.D.M.S.
30. "Q"
31. War Diary.
32. File.

Map E3 will be issued later to recipients of Maps E1 and E2.

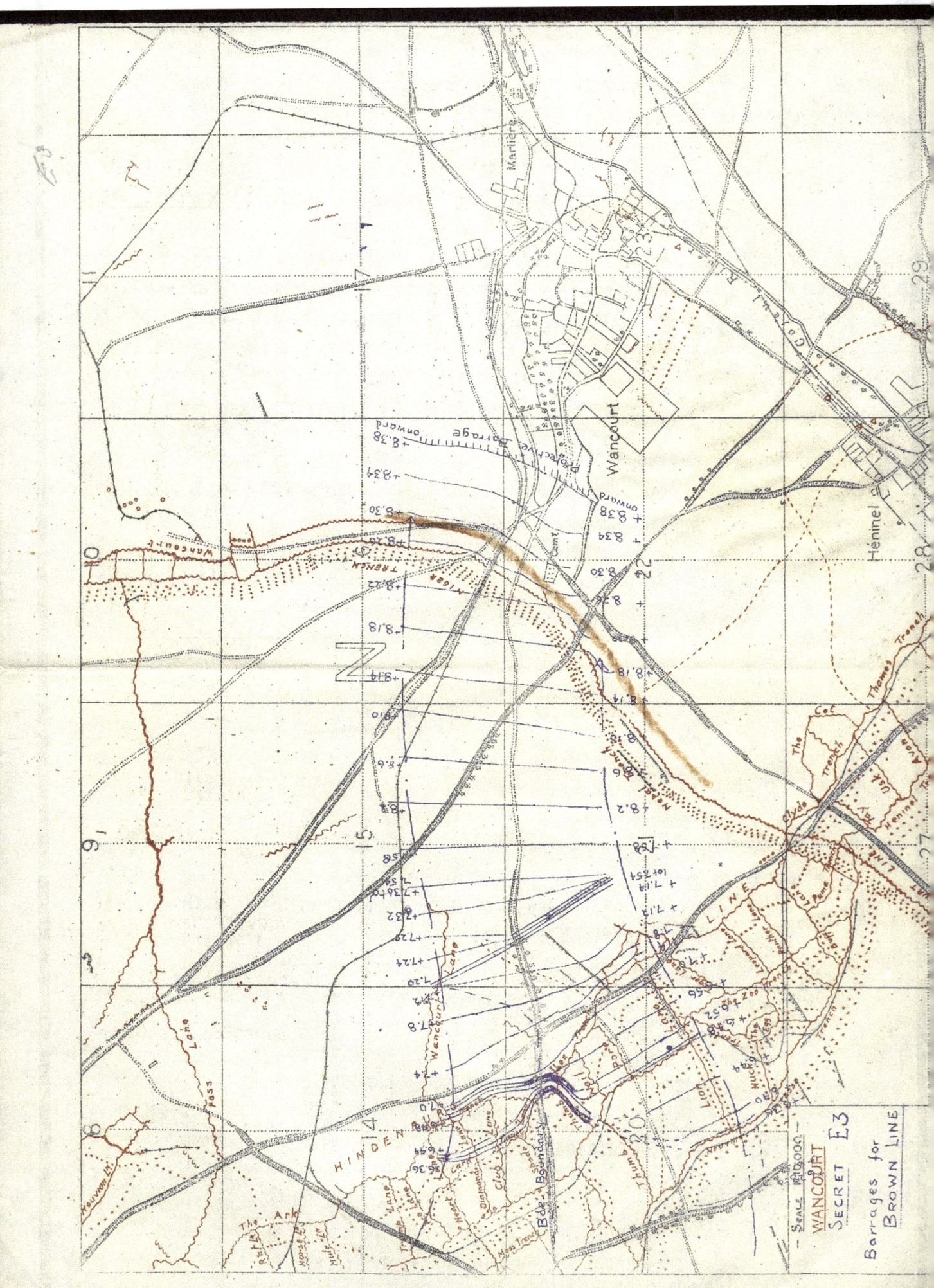

MAP 'F'

Identification Trace for use with Artillery Maps. AREAS FOR REFORMING.

N

56 169
168
167

Tracing taken from Sheet
of the 1 map of
Signature Date

G.S.G.S. 3025.

E1.

NEUVILLE VITASSE

1. Brickfields.
2. Stone built, solid Chateau.
3. Very solid stone house.
4. Solid stone farm, with outhouses of brick, 18m. thick.
5. Big stone house.
6. Watering place.
7. Large solid brick and stone house.
8. Chateau and farm, former brick, latter stone, very strong.
9. Sugar factory, of brick, very solid.
10. Mairie, stone, very solid.
11. Watering place.
12. Big Chateau, with stables, outhouses, brick and stone, very strong.
13. Big stone built farm.
14. Large solid house, of stone.
15. Stone and brick Chateau.
16. Distillery, of brick, solid.
17. Chateau, brick, solid.
18. Big, solid, brick house.
19. Ditto.
20. Old windmill, with walls 2.35m. thick, very strong.
21. Church, with tower, strongly built.
22. Farm, large, of brick and stone, walls standing.
23. Farm, of brick, standing.
24. Brick building, solid.
25. Ditto.

WELLS.—Nearly every house has one (windlass) in its yard or just outside. Average depth 85m.

UNDERGROUND PASSAGES.—Deep and wide under house and grounds of pt. 12. Reported wide enough for cart and horse to drive along. Another reported connecting pts. 7 and 12.

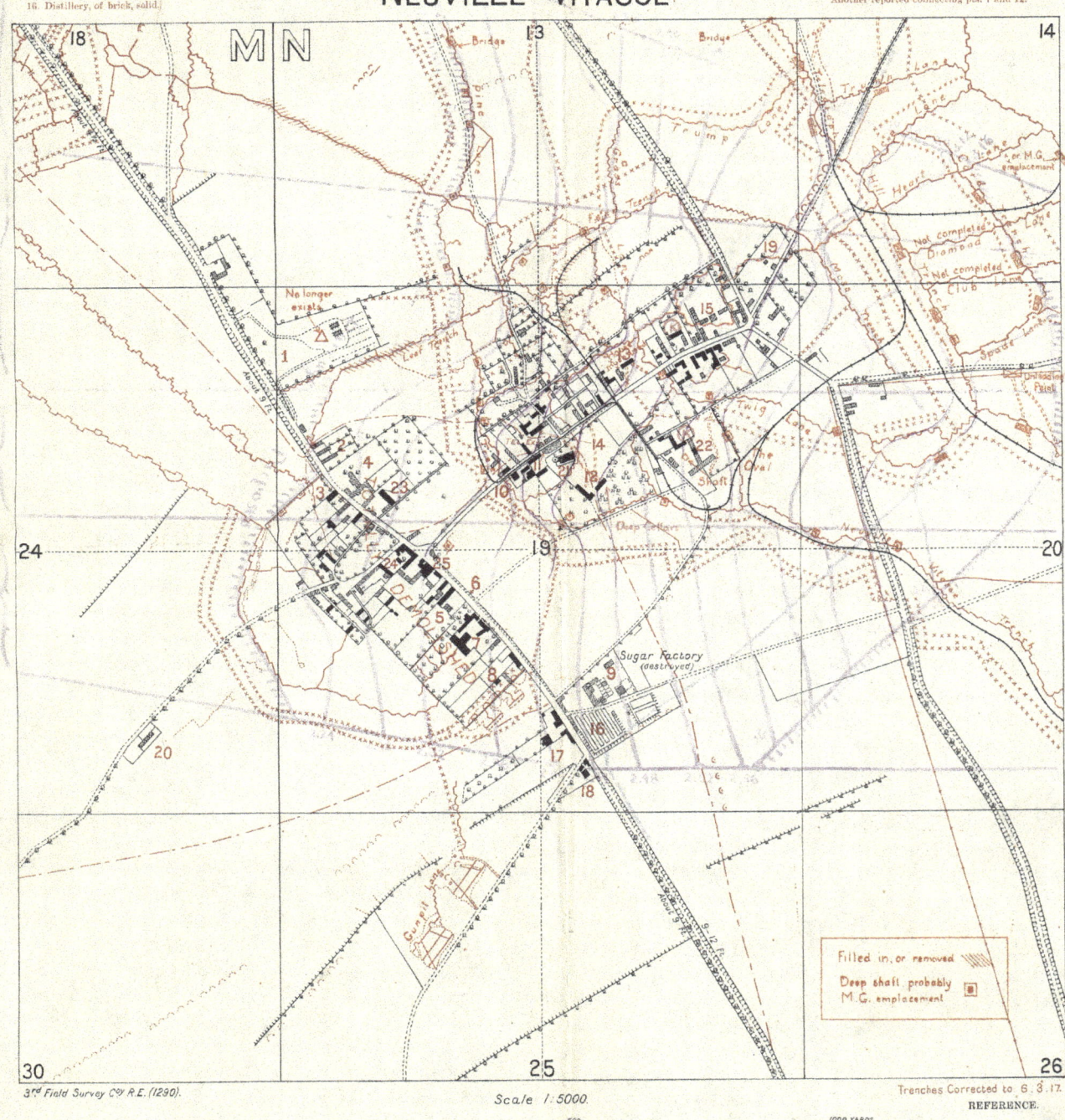

3rd Field Survey Coy R.E. (1290). Scale 1:5000. Trenches Corrected to 6.3.17.

REFERENCE.
- Buildings roofed and apparently complete.
- Buildings partly or wholly demolished.
- △ Dumps.
- O.P's.
- Trench Mortars.
- Good Cellars or Dug-outs.
- M.G. Emplacements.

"A" Form.
MESSAGES AND SIGNALS.

Army Form C. 2121
(in pads of 100).

Prefix......Code......m	Words	Charge	This message is on a/c of:	Recd. at......m
Office of Origin and Service Instructions.				Date..................
copy	Sent At......m		..............Service.	From..................
	To		(Signature of "Franking Officer.")	By..................
	By			

TO { ✓ 167
      ✓ 168
      ✓ 169   ✓ CRA

| Sender's Number. | Day of Month. | In reply to Number. | A A A |
| *G.593 | 10/4 | | |

reference Div. Operation Order No 81 the assault is to be delivered at 12 noon today AAA acknowledge

G/S

From 56 Div
Place
Time 8.22 a.m.

Censor.   (Z) *signature*

"A" Form.
MESSAGES AND SIGNALS.

Army Form C. 2121
(in pads of 100).
No of Message ....

Prefix .... Code .... m | Words | Charge | This message is on a/c of: | Recd. at .... m
Office of Origin and Service Instructions. | Sent | | | Date ....
War Diary | At .... m | | .... Service. | From ....
| To | | S.D.R. |
SECRET | By | | (Signature of "Franking Officer.") | By ....

TO: 167 - 168 - 169 Bdes - 21st - 33rd - 50th Divns - VII Corps.
CRA - CRE - 1/5 Ches Regt. 193rd Div MG Offr - 56th Div Signals
56th Div MG Offr - Adms - Q - War Diary - File

| Sender's Number. | Day of Month. | In reply to Number. | AAA |
| G.763. | 13/4 | | |

~~Operation Order No. 82~~ AAA VIIth Corps will advance
~~to-morrow~~ simultaneously with VIth Corps AAA First
objective line through T.6.b.0.5. - N.36.d.6.0 -
~~road junction~~ O.25.b.7.8. - East edge of Wood in
O.19.d. - O.19.b.9.4. - O.14.c.3.0. AAA Second
objective Sunken Road T.12.b.2.0. through U.1.b.8.0
to CHERISY - CHERISY VILLAGE inclusive - along
~~dotted track to railway crossing at O.27.a.9.7.~~
thence to O.21. central AAA Dividing line between
~~21st and~~ 56th Divisions from present junction road
junction O.31.c.3.6. to North edge of Wood in U.2.a.
AAA Between 56th and 50th Divisions from present
~~junction~~ through Bench mark O.25.b.5.5. and
~~Northern~~ end of CHERISY VILLAGE AAA Successive
objectives will be consolidated and posts pushed
forward from final objective to about the line of
~~of~~ the railway along the SENSEE VALLEY AAA Advance
will be made under rolling barrage at rate 100 yds.
in four minutes AAA At junction of VI and VII Corps
barrage will stop in front of first objective at
~~Zero plus 44 mins and move~~ forward again at Zero
plus 60 AAA C.R.A. will communicate barrage and
bombardment details direct to G.O.C. 169th Inf.Bde.

From			
Place			
Time			

The above may be forwarded as now corrected. (Z)

.... Censor. | Signature of Addressor or person authorised to telegraph in his name
* This line should be erased if not required.
100,000 Pads. W. 12093. M1217. McC. & Co., Ltd. 1/17. (E. 764). Forms C/2121/11.

"A" Form.
MESSAGES AND SIGNALS.

Army Form C. 2121
(in pads of 100).
No of Message..........

Prefix......Code.........m.	Words	Charge	This message is on a/c of:	Recd. at............m.
Office of Origin and Service Instructions.	Sent		...............Service.	Date................
....	At.........m.			From................
....	To........		(Signature of "Franking Officer.")	By..................
	By........			

TO {

Sender's Number. | Day of Month. | In reply to Number. | AAA

AAA The attack will be carried out by 169th Inf.
Bde. AAA Zero hour will be 5.30 a.m. tomorrow AAA
A contact 'plane will be in the air during the
operations AAA Patrolling will be active tonight
AAA ACKNOWLEDGE AAA Addressed 167th, 168th, 169th
Brigades, 21st 33rd and 50th Divisions VII Corps
C.R.A. C.R.E. 5th Cheshire Regt. 193rd Div. M.G.Coy.
56th Div. M.G.Officer, Signals, A.D.M.S. and Q.

From
Place 56th Division.
Time 10.10 pm

The above may be forwarded as now corrected.   (Z).

Censor.   General Staff.
Signature of Addressor or person authorised to telegraph in his name

*This line should be erased if not required.
100,000 Pads. W.12093. M1217. McC. & Co., Ltd. 1/17. (E. 764). Forms C/2121/1L.

"A" Form.
MESSAGES AND SIGNALS.

Army Form C. 2121
(in pads of 100).
No of Message ....

Prefix... Code... m.	Words.	Charge	This message is on a/c of:	Recd. at .... m.
Office of Origin and Service Instructions.			SDR	Date ....
	Sent			From ....
	At ..... m.		Service.	
	To			
	By		(Signature of "Franking Officer.")	By ....

TO: 167, 168, 169 Bdes 193rd Div. M.G. Coy. 56th Div. M.G Off 33 & 50th Divns VII Corps CRA, CRE, 1/5 Ches. Regt. Signals, ADMS "Q" 56th Dw. Train Way Diary File.

Sender's Number.	Day of Month.	In reply to Number.	
* G.862.	17		A A A

Operation Order No. 83 AAA NUB will relieve LOB in the line on the night 17/18th April AAA Two Battalions of KEB will come under Orders of NUB from the commencement of the relief to-morrow and will be accommodated forward in NUB'S present area, their place in KEB'S area being taken by support and reserve Battalions of LOB AAA H.Q. and remaining Battalions of LOB will return to NUB'S present area AAA The two Sections Div.M.G.Coy. at present under orders of LOB will come under orders of NUB from completion of relief AAA Brigadiers will arrange all details direct AAA ACKNOWLEDGE AAA Addressed 167th 168th 169th Brigades 33rd & 50th Divisions VII Corps C.R.A. C.R.E.1/5th Cheshire Regiment, 193rd Div. M.G.Company, 56th Div. Signals, 56th Div. M.G.Officer, A.D.M.S. "Q" & 56th Div. Train.

From 56th Divn.
Place
Time

The above may be forwarded as now corrected. (Z)

(Sgd.) B. PAKENHAM,
Lt. Col. G.S.

"A" Form.
MESSAGES AND SIGNALS.

Army Form C. 2121
(in pads of 100).
No. of Message ....

Priority
Pakenham Lt Col

TO: 167 Bde
168 —
169 —

Sender's Number: G 867
Day of Month: 1/4

AAA

No action should be taken on Div Order No 83 issued this evening until further orders Hull aaa AAA addsd 167, 168 + 169 Bdes & Q

From: 56th Div
Place:
Time: 7.35 pm

(Z) B Pakenham Lt Col

"A" Form.
MESSAGES AND SIGNALS.
Army Form C. 2121 (in pads of 100).

Prefix ...... Code ...... m	Words	Charge	This message is on a/c of:	Recd. at ...... m
Office of Origin and Service Instructions.	Sent			Date......
War	At ...... m		Service.	From......
SDR to IO	To		(Signature of "Franking Officer.")	By......
	By			

TO { To all recipients of order No 84

Sender's Number. | Day of Month. | In reply to Number. | AAA

Reference 56th Division Order No. 84 of 19th inst destinations of Brigades on relief are altered as follows AAA HUB will proceed to POMMIER Area AAA LOB to COUIN Area AAA and KMP to SOUASTRE Area AAA Destinations of Field Coys. R.E. Field Ambulances and Train Coys. will be altered accordingly AAA ACKNOWLEDGE AAA Addressed all recipients of Order No. 84.

From   56th Divn.
Place
Time   11.45 pm

General Staff.

The above may be forwarded as now corrected.   (Z)

SECRET.   Copy No. 25

56th DIVISION ORDER NO. 84.

18th April 1917.

1. 56th Division Order No. 83 is cancelled.

2. 30th Division is to relieve 56th Division (less artillery).

3. 90th Infantry Brigade relieves 167th Infantry Brigade to-day.

    167th Infantry Brigade on relief will proceed TO ARRAS, and will proceed to COUIN Area to-morrow by 'bus.

    Arrangements for embussing will be issued by "Q".

4. On 19th inst :-

    21st Infantry Brigade relieves 90th Infantry Brigade.

    90th Infantry Brigade relieves 168th Infantry Brigade (plus attached Battalion of 169th Infantry Brigade).

    168th Infantry Brigade will proceed to ARRAS on relief. Attached Battalion 169th Infantry Brigade will rejoin its Brigade.

    168th Infantry Brigade will proceed by 'bus from ARRAS to SOUASTRE Area on 21st instant under arrangements to be communicated later.

5. On 20th inst :-

    89th Infantry Brigade relieves 169th Infantry Brigade.

    169th Infantry Brigade will proceed to POMMIER Area by 'bus under arrangements to be communicated later.

6. Pioneer Battalion of 30th Division will relieve 1/5th Cheshire Regiment (Pioneers) on afternoon of 19th instant.

    On relief, latter will proceed to WAILLY, and on 20th instant will march to ST.AMAND.

7. Field Coys. R.E. will be located with their affiliated Infantry Brigades after relief:-

    416th Field Coy. will concentrate at ACHICOURT tonight & march to COUIN Area on 19th instant.

    512th Field Coy. will concentrate at AGNY on 19th and march to SOUASTRE Area on 20th instant.

    513th Field Coy. will concentrate at ACHICOURT on 19th and march to POMMIER Area on 20th instant.

8. The 56th Divisional Artillery will come under the orders of G.O.C. 30th Division at 3 p.m. 19th instant.

9. Details of relief will be settled direct between Brigadiers concerned.

    G.O.C. 168th Infantry Brigade will leave 168th M.G.Coy. and the attached two Sections 193rd Div. M.G.Coy. in the line to be relieved during the day of 20th and night 20th/21st April.

    He will also arrange to leave 1 Officer per Company and 1 N.C.O. per platoon with 90th Infantry Brigade until midday 20th instant.

P.T.O.   /10.

- 2 -

10.   Orders for relief of 193rd Div. M.G.Coy. will be issued later.

11.   Train Coys. will march under the orders of O.C., Div. Train.

12.   Orders for moves of Medical and Veterinary Units will be issued later.

13.   Divisional H.Q. will close at its present location at 3 p.m. 19th inst., and will then open at POMMIER.

14.   ACKNOWLEDGE.

B Pakenham

Head Qrs. 56th Divn.   Lieut-Colonel,
                                        General Staff.

Issued at 2.30pm

Copy No. 1. 167th Infantry Brigade.
        2.   168th Infantry Brigade.
        3.   169th Infantry Brigade.
        4.   VII Corps.
        5.   30th Division.
        6.   33rd Division.
        7.   50th Division.
        8.   1/5th Cheshire Regt.
        9.   C.R.A.
        10. C.R.E.
        11. A.P.M.
        12. 193rd Div. M.G.Coy.
        13. 56th Div. Signals.
        14. 56th Div. Train.
        15. 56th Div. M.G.Officer.
        16. 56th Div. Gas Officer.
        17. D.A.D.O.S.
        18. 4th Aust. Div. Supply Column.
        19. No. 2 Ammn. Sub Park.
        20. A.D.M.S.
        21. A.D.V.S.
        22. "Q"
        23. G.O.C.
        24. A.D.C.
        25. War Diary.
        26. File.

"A" Form.
MESSAGES AND SIGNALS.

Army Form C. 2121
(in pads of 100).
No of Message ....

Prefix	Code	m	Words	Charge	This message is on a/c of:	Recd. at .... m.
			Sent			Date
			At .... m.		.... Service.	From
			To			
			By		(Signature of "Franking Officer.")	By

TO
- 167 Bde / 5 Ches Regt / 56th Div Signals / 2 Aux Div Sup Col / Sup Col
- 168 " / CRA / " Train / No 2 Am Sub Park /
- 169 " / CRE / " MG Offr / ADMS / GOC
- XVIII Corps / ADM / Gas Offr / ADVS / AA & QMG
- 193 Dw MG Cy / SAA Col / Q / Gen Staff

| Sender's Number. | Day of Month. | In reply to Number. | |
| O.983 | 24/4 | | A A A |

56th Div. Order No. 35 AAA 169th Brigade Group will move to-day from SOUASTRE Area to WANQUETIN via BIENVILLERS - BAILLEULVAL - SIMENCOURT AAA To be clear of present area by 2 p.m. AAA 168th Brigade Group will move to day from COUIN Area to GOUY via SOUASTRE - LAHERLIERE - HAVINCOURT AAA Not to enter SOUASTRE before 2.30 p.m. AAA Moves to be complete by 6 p.m. AAA Intervals 800 yards between battalions or between battalions and transport AAA Intervals 200 yards between sections of transport if brigaded AAA 167th Brigade will be prepared to move to-morrow morning by busses AAA Other Divisional troops will be prepared to move to-day at short notice AAA ACKNOWLEDGE AAA Added all recipients of Orders.

From	56th Divn.		
Place			
Time	11.40 am		

The above may be forwarded as now corrected. (Z)
.... General Staff.
Censor. Signature of Addressor or person authorised to telegraph in his name.
* This line should be erased if not required.

SECRET. Copy No. 24

56th DIVISION ORDER No. 86.

26th April, 1917.

Reference 1/40,000 Map - Sheet 51B and 51C.

1. 56th Division is to relieve 15th Division in the Line and has now come under the orders of VI Corps.

2. The relief will be carried out as follows :-

   27th inst. and night 27th/28th inst.

   167th Infantry Brigade will relieve 46th Infantry Brigade (15th Division Reserve Brigade at present in the Support Brigade Area) Headquarters at H.31 central.

   28th inst. and night 28th/29th inst.

   169th Infantry Brigade will relieve 167th Infantry Brigade.
   167th Infantry Brigade will relieve 44th & 45th Infantry Brigades in the Line.
   H.Q. of 44th Infantry Brigade - N.16.b.18.
   H.Q. of 45th Infantry Brigade - N.10.d.37.

   168th Infantry Brigade will march to ARRAS and become Divisional Reserve.

3. The above Units will come under the orders of General Officer Commanding 15th Division on leaving their present areas.

4. The relief of R.E. Companies and Pioneer Battalions will be arranged between the C.R.E's 56th & 15th Divisions.

5. The A.D.M.S. will carry out the necessary reliefs of Medical Units.

6. Moves will be carried out in accordance with the attached March Table.

7. All details of relief will be settled between Brigadiers concerned.

8. 15th Division are arranging to leave behind for a maximum period of 24 hours :-

   1 Officer-per Battalion of 167th Infantry Brigade.
   1 N.C.O. -per Company of 167th Infantry Brigade.

9. Two Sections of 193rd Div. M.G.Coy. will be placed at the disposal of 167th Infantry Brigade. 193rd Div. M.G.Coy. H.Q. and Section at AGNEZ-LES-DUISANS, and the 3 Sections detached at FOSSEUX, SAULTY & BEAUMETZ respectively will concentrate at DAINVILLE at 2 p.m. to-morrow.
   The Coy. will then proceed to ARRAS where it will billet under orders to be issued by "Q".
   O.C. Coy. will report to G.O.C. 167th Infantry Brigade for orders at H.31 central at 10 a.m. 28th instant.

10. General Officer Commanding 56th Division will assume command of the line at 10 a.m. 29th inst.

/11

- 2 -

11. Div. H.Q. will close at WARLUS at 10 a.m. 29th inst. and open at 15, Rue de la Paix, ARRAS, at the same hour.

12. ACKNOWLEDGE.

B Pakenham

Head Qrs. 56th Divn.

Lieut-Colonel,
General Staff.

Issued at 8.45 p.m.

Copy :-
No. 1. 167th Infantry Brigade.
2. 168th Infantry Brigade.
3. 169th Infantry Brigade.
4. 15th Division.
5. VI Corps.
6. 3rd Division.
7. 1/5th Cheshire Regiment.
8. C.R.A.
9. C.R.E.
10. A.P.M.
11. 193rd Div. M.G.Coy.
12. 56th Div. Signals.
13. 56th Div. Train.
14. 56th Div. M.G.Officer.
15. 56th Div. Gas Officer.
16. D.A.D.O.S.
17. 4th Aust. Div. Supply Column.
18. No. 2 Ammn. Sub Park.
19. A.D.M.S.
20. A.D.V.S.
21. "Q"
22. G.O.C.
23. A.D.C.
24. War Diary.
25. File.
26. 14th Division.

MARCH TABLE ISSUED WITH 56th DIVISION ORDER No.86.

Date.	Unit.	From	To	In relief of	Route and Remarks.
27th April.	167th Inf.Bde.	DUISANS.	Support Brigade Area 15th Division.	46th Infantry Bde.	Under arrangements to be made by G.O.C. 167th Inf.Bde. No restrictions as to route or time.
28th April.	169th Inf.Bde.	BERNEVILLE.	Support Brigade Area.	167th Infantry Bde.	via DAINVILLE. To be clear of cross roads L.35.b. by 4 p.m.
	168th Inf.Bde.	SIMENCOURT.	ARRAS.		via BERNEVILLE & DAINVILLE. Not to pass cross roads L.35.b. before 4 p.m.

On the march W. of ARRAS the following distances will be observed between Units :-

    Between Battalions 500 yards.

        "   Coys.   200 yards.

        "   Sections of transport or between transport & battalions 200 yards.

E. of ARRAS distances will be kept in accordance with tactical requirements.

SECRET.   Copy No. 26

56th DIVISION WARNING ORDER No. 87.
                                                                        29th April '17.

Reference 1/20,000 Map - Sheet 51 B. S.W. Edition 4a.

1. A general attack is to be carried out by the Fifth, Third & First Armies on 3rd May.

2. The objective of VII Corps on our right will probably include the Village of CHERISY and the trenches in O.21.

   The objective of 3rd Division on our left will include the BOIS DU VERT, and the continuation of the ridge running North to the BOIS DU SART.

3. The objective of 56th Division is the ridge running North from ST.ROHART Factory (inclusive) to about O.9.b.9.0.

   A map showing inter Brigade and Divisional Boundaries and Assembly Areas is attached (A).

4. The attack will be carried out by 169th Infantry Brigade on the right, and by 167th Infantry Brigade on the left.
   168th Infantry Brigade will be in Divisional Reserve.

5. Arrangements will be made for co-operation by the Div. M.G.Coy. with a view to enfilading the hostile trenches from positions on the right bank of the COJEUL RIVER, and to barraging all suspected M.G. emplacements in the open.

6. The Artillery will form two lines of barrage :-

   (a) A creeping barrage close in front of the Infantry with 2/3 of the 18-pdrs. available.

   (b) A sweeping barrage, in front of the creeping barrage, with 1/3 of the 18-pdrs. available, a proportion firing smoke shell, and a proportion of 4.5" Hows.

   (c) 4.5"s not employed in the sweeping barrage are to be employed on counter-battery work.

   (d) 60 Pdrs. firing shrapnel are to be directed on selected points from which Machine Gun fire is likely, e.g. ST.ROHART Factory, mounds in BOIS DU VERT.
   Any other special points which Brigadiers wish to be specially treated are to be reported to Div. H.Q.

7. The rate of the barrage will be 100 yards in 3 minutes, except where there are strong hostile systems or features such as woods or villages likely to cause delay.

8. 169th Infantry Brigade will take over the Right Brigade Section to-night, with Brigade H.Q. a/N.16.a.18.

9. General Officers Commanding 167th and 169th Infantry Brigades will arrange to relieve to-night the two Sections 193rd Div. M.G.Coy. at present attached to 167th Infantry Brigade. These Sections will then rejoin their Company.

10. ACKNOWLEDGE.

                                                       B Pakenham
Head Qrs. 56th Divn.   Lieut-Colonel,
                                                       General Staff.
          Issued at 2.30 p.m.

                                                                        P.T.O.

- 2 -

```
Copy No.  1. 167th Infantry Brigade.
          2. 168th Infantry Brigade.
          3. 169th Infantry Brigade.
        * 4. 3rd Division.
        * 5. 14th Division.
          6. VI Corps H.A.
          7.  "    "   Artillery.
          8. No. 12 Squadron R.F.C.
          9. 1/5th Cheshire Regt.
         10. C.R.A.
         11. C.R.E.
        *12. A.P.M.
         13. 193rd Div. M.G.Coy.
         14. 56th Div. Signals.
        *15. 56th Div. Train.
         16. 56th Div. M.G.Officer.
        *17. 56th Div. Gas Officer.
        *18. D.A.D.O.S.
        *19. 4th Aust. Div. Supply Column.
        *20. No. 2 Ammn. Sub Park.
         21. A.D.M.S.
        *22. A.D.V.S.
         23. "Q"
        *24. G.O.C.
        *25. A.D.C.
         26. War Diary.
         27. File.
```

* Map not attached.

SECRET. Copy No. 26

56th DIVISION ORDER No. 88   30th April, 1917

1. The Fifth, Third and First Armies are to attack simultaneously on "Z" day, the main objective being a line FONTAINE LES CROISILLES - CHERISY - ST ROHART FACTORY - BOIS DU VERT - BOIS DU SART - PLOUVAIN Station - Square Wood (C.27.c.).

2. The object of the VI Corps is to capture and consolidate the RED LINE as shown on the attached Map "B". The tracing (A) issued with 56th Div. Warning Order No. 87 of 29th inst. is cancelled.

3. The 3rd Division will be on the left of 56th Division. The 14th Division (VII Corps) will be on the right.

4. The objective of 56th Division is the RED LINE within the Divisional Boundaries.

5. The attack will be carried out by 169th Infantry Brigade on the right, and by 167th Infantry Brigade on the left.
    The dividing line between Brigades and the areas allotted for their assembly are shown on the attached map "B".
    The magnetic bearing of the dividing line is approximately 103 degrees.

6. As soon as the RED LINE is captured it will be consolidated and patrols, supported by formed bodies of Infantry, will be pushed forward in order to gain ground towards the GREEN LINE shown on the attached map.

    The first objective of these patrols will be an approximate line O.10.b.90. - SENSEE RIVER - PONT A TROIS GUEULES.

    According as the troops on our right and left progress & make good VIS EN ARTOIS and the high ground about BOIRY NOTRE DAME, those patrols will push further forward to approximately the line O.11.a.40. - bridge O.11.c.54. - the Sunken Road O.17.a. & c.
    These patrols must be supplied with means of Visual communications.

7. (a). The whole of the Artillery will be under the G.O.C. R.A. VI Corps and artillery instructions will be issued separately.

    (b). The creeping barrage will advance at the rate of 100 yds. in 3 minutes, except through the Woods where it will advance at the rate of 100 yds. in 6 minutes.

    (c). Prior to "Z" day heavy and siege artillery will continue to bombard the enemy's positions and to carry out counter-battery work.

    (d). On X/Y and Y/Z nights the enemy's battery positions and woods will be shelled with gas shells. Gas shells will not be thrown into the woods after Zero minus 6 hours.

8. On "Z" day, No. 12 Squadron, R.F.C. is to provide two contact machines to be over the front as soon as light is sufficiently good for observation.
    After 7 a.m. only one contact machine will be maintained over the line.

9. Flares will be called for at 6 a.m. by the contact aeroplanes by sounding Klaxon Horns or by firing white lights.
    Flares will not be lit until called for.

- 2 -

10. 167th and 169th Infantry Brigades will be closed up into their concentration areas East of and including the WANCOURT LINE by 11 p.m. on "Y" day.

11. 168th Infantry Brigade will be clear of ARRAS by 8 p.m. on "Y" day.

H.Q. will be established at H.31 central and units will be accommodated between the WANCOURT LINE (exclusive) and the old German front line (inclusive) within the Divisional boundaries, with the two leading Battalions about N.2.c. and d.

As and when G.Os.C. 167th and 169th Infantry Brigades move forward their Reserve Battalions from the WANCOURT LINE, they will inform G.O.C. 168th Infantry Brigade, who will move up Battalions to take their place.

12. G.O.C. 168th Infantry Brigade will arrange to carry out reconnaissances with a view to the advance of his Brigade to the dotted GREEN or GREEN LINES, should it be called upon.

As this advance might take place after dark all arrangements should be made accordingly and compass bearings taken.

13. Orders for the employment of certain machine guns for barrage work and for enfilading hostile trenches will be issued later.

14. The following R.E. and Pioneers will be allotted to 167th and 169th Infantry Brigades for the operations:-

167th Infantry Brigade - 416th Field Coy.R.E.(less 2 Sections)
1 Coy. 5th Ches. Regt.(Pioneers)

169th Infantry Brigade - 2 Sections 416th Fld.Coy. R.E.
1 Coy. 5th Ches. Regt.(Pioneers)

Arrangements will be made by the C.R.E. to attach two Sections R.E. and one Coy Pioneers to 168th Infantry Bde. in the event of the latter being ordered to carry on the advance beyond the RED LINE.

15. The A.D.M.S. will make the necessary medical arrangements.

16. "Z" day and Zero hour will be notified later.

17. Div. H.Q. will remain at 15. Rue de la PAIX, ARRAS,

18. ACKNOWLEDGE.

B Pakenham
Lieut-Colonel,
General Staff.

Head Qrs. 56th Divn.

Issued at 1 p.m.

Copy No.			
1. 167th Inf.Bde.	10. C.R.A.	*19. 4th Aust.D.
2. 168th Inf.Bde.	11. C.R.E.	*20 No.2 A.S.Pk
3. 169th Inf.Bde.	*12. A.P.M.	*21. A.D.M.S.
*4. 3rd Division.	13. 193rd Div.M.G.C.	*22. A.D.V.S.
*5. 14th Division.	14. 56th Div.Signals.	23. "Q"
6. VI Corps H.A.	15. 56th Div. Train.	*24. G.O.C.
7. VI Corps Arty.	16. 56th Div. M.G.O.	*25. A.D.C.
8. No.12. Squad.R.F.C.	*17 56th Div. Gas Off.	26. War Diary.
9. 1/5th Ches.Regt.	*18.D.A.D.O.S.	27. File.

* Map not attached.

SECRET.   56th Divn. G.A.234.

VII Corps.   C.R.E.
 " Artillery.   1/5th Cheshire Regt.
 " Heavy Arty.   193rd Div. M.G.Coy.
 " M.G.Officer.   56th Div.M.G.Officer.
1st Bde. H.B.M.G.Corps.   G.O.C.
"D" Bn.   "   "   "   A.D.C.
14th Division.   War Diary.
30th Division.   File.
No. 8 Squadron R.F.C.   Lieut.BELL, c/o "D"Bn.H.B.M.G.C.
C.R.A.

In continuation of 56th Division Orders Nos.79 and 80 -

Herewith Map E3 showing Barrages from BLUE to BROWN

LINE.

    NOTE. - Eastern end of 56th Divisional Northern
           Boundary is shown too far to the N.; it
           should meet BROWN LINE at N.16.c.95.50. of
           Map "C" issued with Divisional Order No. 79.
           This does not, however, affect the "lifts" of
           barrage as shown in purple.

Head Qrs. 56th Divn.   L.A. Newnham Capt
7th April, 1917.   for Lieut-Colonel,
                                             General Staff.

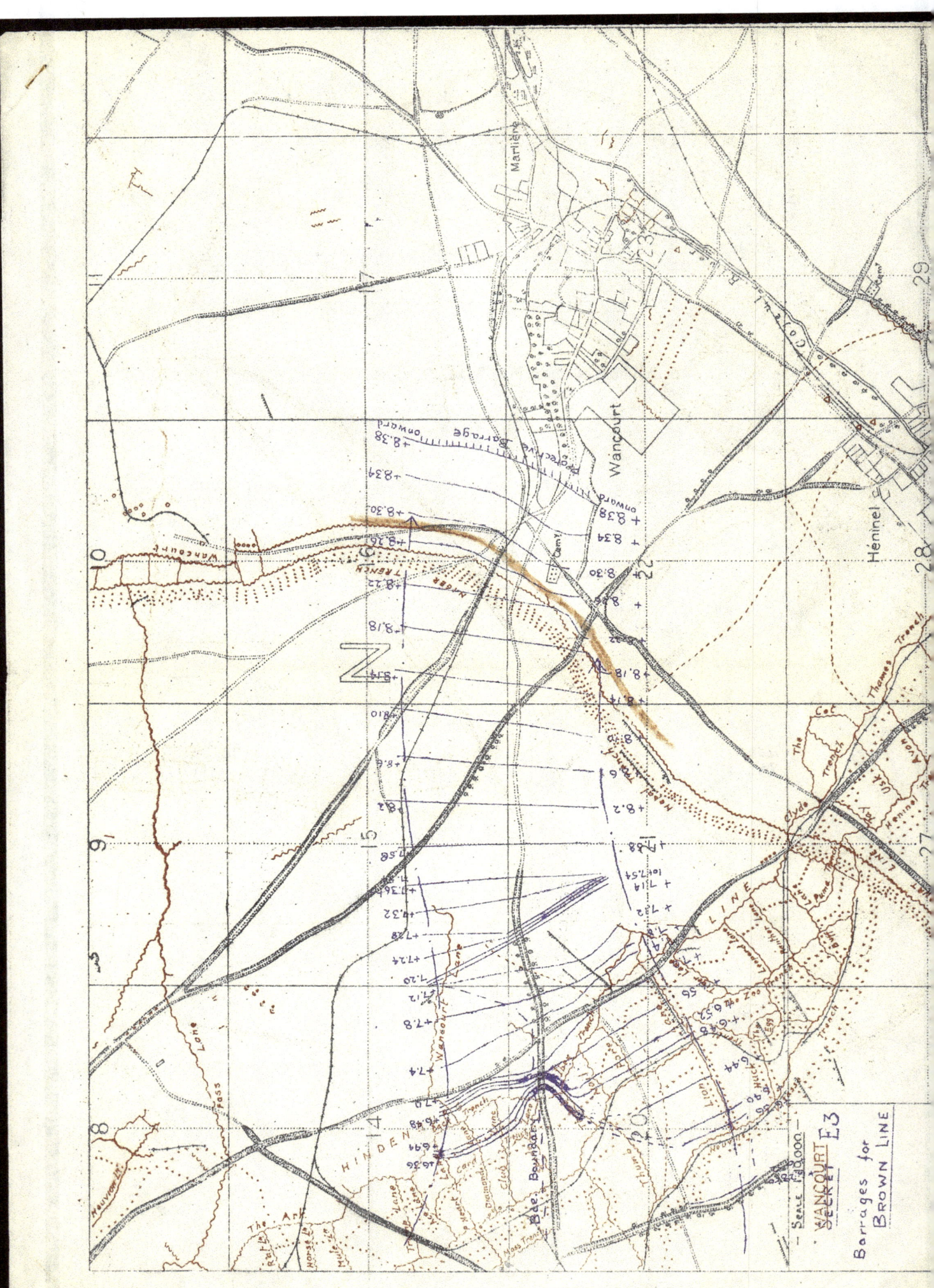

"A" Form.
MESSAGES AND SIGNALS.

Army Form C. 2121 (in pads of 100).

TO: 169 Bde 167 Bde

Sender's Number: G 565   Day of Month: 9

AAA

You will place one battalion under the orders of 167 Bde aaa This Bde will report to 167 Bde at HQ for orders at once aaa added 169 Bde reply 167 Bde

From: 56 Dn
Time: 12.45 pm

"A" Form.
MESSAGES AND SIGNALS.

Army Form C. 2121 (in pads of 100).

TO	167 Bde
	168 Bde
	169 Bde

B

Sender's Number.	Day of Month.	In reply to Number.	AAA
G 586	9/6		

Corps wires before AAA spirit and movement of advance from Blue dum AAA It is important to press enemy leaving any strong posts holding out to be dealt with by parties in rear AAA Time table should be adhered to AAA ends AAA added NYR and LRB rpld KEB

From 56 Div
Place
Time 1.15 pm

"A" Form.
MESSAGES AND SIGNALS.

Army Form C. 2121 (in pads of 100).

TO 167 Bde
168

Sender's Number: G 572
Day of Month: 9/4
AAA

NVB will push forward the three companies of WHEAT through LOSK to support CROWN moving them North of the NEUVILLE-VITASSE WANCOURT road AAA [illegible] CROWN and WHEAT will then push forward in touch with 14th Div to gain line of new trench N.22.a.0? - N.15.d.26. AAA addsd NVB refsd LOB.

From: 56 Div
Place:
Time: 4.20 pm

B Pakenham Lt Col

"A" Form.
MESSAGES AND SIGNALS.

Army Form C. 2121 (in pads of 100).

Priority LOKinhy

TO VII Corps   D/

Sender's Number.	Day of Month.	In reply to Number.	AAA
G 585	10th	G 532	

Situation of this Division ordinally 10 pm AAA gather understood the enemy were at IBEX THUMB in trench from junction of Lane and also THUMB TELEGRAPH trenches in to junction with Parties of trench HILL trench AAA RAIL and Enemy also in we hold a PORE trenches AAA and TELEGRAPH HILL trench not and line 200 yards LION LANE parallel to LION recovered trench AAA Reports just towards that Enemy are Reinforcing Sunken trenches in 21 a & c up road from direction of the

From KITTY
Place
Time 12.40 AM   Cont

"A" Form.
MESSAGES AND SIGNALS.

Army Form C. 2121
(in pads of 100).
No of Message..........

Prefix....Code....m	Words	Charge	This message is on a/c of:	Recd. at....m
Office of Origin and Service Instructions.	Sent		...............Service.	Date............
	At....m			From............
	To			
	By	(2)	(Signature of "Franking Officer.")	By............

TO { VII Corps.   Cont

Sender's Number.	Day of Month.	In reply to Number.	AAA

WANCOURT line AAA arrangements have been made to drive the enemy out of the various points he holds in the COJEUL switch until this has been done and correction obtained with 14th Division on our left orders caught in accordance with issued situation G562 AAA be your not likely to is up before daybreak cleared

From: Kitty
Place:
Time: 12.15 am

The above may be forwarded as now corrected. (Z)

"A" Form.
MESSAGES AND SIGNALS.

Army Form C. 2121 (in pads of 100).

TO	AUB ~~KER~~	KER		E

Sender's Number.	Day of Month.	In reply to Number.	AAA
* G 596	10		

Batta of KEB now in old German front line is placed at disposal of NUB and C.O. of this Batta to report to NUB HQ at once & Batta to move to trenches now occupied by DICK and MISS KEB reply NUB

From KITTY
Place
Time 9.16 AM

(Z) Lawrenley

PRIORITY

"A" Form.
MESSAGES AND SIGNALS.

Army Form C. 2121
(in pads of 100).
No of Message ....

Prefix .... Code .... m | Words | Charge
Office of Origin and Service Instructions.

This message is on a/c of:

Recd. at .... m.
Date ....

PRIORITY
167th Bde.

Sent
At .... m.
To ....
By ....

.... Service.

(Signature of "Franking Officer.")

From ....
By ....

TO: 167th Bde.   C.R.A.
~~168th Bde.~~
~~169th Bde.~~

Sender's Number.   Day of Month.   In reply to Number.
* G.605   10   AAA

~~Enemy apparently withdrawing from BROWN LINE~~ part
of VI corps being already through it on NORTH AAA
After the capture of BROWN LINE as ordered in
56th Div. O. No. 81 advance will be continued to
GREEN LINE AAA Objectives of Divisions as follows
AAA   14th Div. WANCOURT and high ground about
N.24 AAA 30th Division HENINEL and high ground
about N.29.b. AAA   21st Div. high ground in N.35
AAA   56th Div. will assist 14th Divn. and 30th
Div by occupying high ground in N.21.d. and N.22.c.
AAA   14th Div. will advance from NIGER TR. when
right Div. of 6th Corps on their left moves forward
from that trench AAA 56th Div. will seize high ground
in N.22.c. simultaneously if they cannot do so earlier
AAA The 30th and 21st Divns. will then work their
way forward AAA The advance must develop from left
AAA   167th Inf.Bde will conform to above orders AAA
Acknowledge.

Place   56th Division.
Time   11.51 a.m.

The above may be forwarded as now corrected.   (Z)
                                                  (Sgd.) B.PAKENHAM,
Censor.   Signature of Addressor or person authorized to telegraph in his name
Lt.Col. G.S.
* This line should be erased if not required.

"A" Form.
MESSAGES AND SIGNALS.

Army Form C. 2121 (in pads of 100).

TO:
167 Bde	CRA	Q
168 Bde	CRE	YEF
169 Bde	Div MG Coy	1/5 Cheshire

6

Sender's Number: G.618
Day of Month: 10

AAA

having obtained its objective NUB will reform in WANCOURT LINE and COJEUL SWITCH trenches South of ~~sunken~~ ~~road~~ NEUVILLE VITASSE — WANCOURT road covered by outposts on high ground in N.21.d and N.22.c and will return battalions of KEB to their Brigade AAA LOB will reform in present position about NEUVILLE VITASSE AAA KEB will reform in area old British and German front lines and trenches in M.17.d and 18.c AAA RAMVIC will concentrate in AGNY AAA Section R.E and Pioneer Corps detached will come under orders of CRE AAA Artillery to remain in present positions teams and limbers returning to existing wagon lines about WAILLY tonight

"A" Form.
MESSAGES AND SIGNALS.

Army Form C. 2121
(in pads of 100).

addsd Inf Bdes CRA CRE RAMVIC Q ~~cont~~ YEF and GROPI

From 56 Div
Place
Time 5.5 pm

(Z) Blakenhay Lt Col

"A" Form.
MESSAGES AND SIGNALS.

Army Form C. 2121 (in pads of 100).

TO: 14th Div.
167 Bde
CRA
H

Sender's Number: G 623
Day of Month: 10

AAA

14th Div. report that high ground in N21d & N22c is still held by Germans & that 14th Div. troops S of WANCOURT cannot advance for this reason aaa Report of FOO that Germans had been seen digging in N22c seems to confirm this aaa Important that you should occupy this ground which enfilades Brown line of 14th Div aaa You will ascertain situation & if Germans are occupying high ground they must be driven out by you tomorrow morning aaa You will make arrangements for artillery support direct with 50 ART aaa Added 167 Bde reptd 14th Div & CRA 56 Div only

From: Kitty
Place:
Time: 8.20 pm

"A" Form.
MESSAGES AND SIGNALS.

Army Form C. 2121 (in pads of 100).

TO: 167 Bde, 7th Corps, 14 Div, 56 Div

Sender's Number: G 625
Day of Month: 10/4

7th Corps wire begins AAA My advance on WANCOURT held up by m.g. fire from HILL 90 N.22.c AAA you are to take point HILL 90 at once in order to assist advance of 14th Div AAA ends AAA you will arrange to make good at once the whole of the objectives which were allotted to you today including the high ground in N.21.d and N.22.c AAA acknowledge AAA address 167 Bde repeat 7th Corps 14 + 56 Divs.

From: 56 Div
Time: 9.5 pm

"A" Form.

MESSAGES AND SIGNALS.

Army Form C. 2121
(in pads of 100).

No of Message..........

Prefix............Code..............m. Office of Origin and Service Instructions.	Words / Charge	This message is on a/c of:	Recd. at..................m
Priority [illegible]	Sent At..................m. To.................. By..................	............................Service. .... (Signature of "Franking Officer.")	Date.................. From.................. By..................

TO 167 / 168 / 169 — CRA [illegible] — I

Sender's Number.	Day of Month.	In reply to Number.	AAA
* G 636	[illegible]		

Confirmation my G 627 and 637 AAA The
Div [illegible] attack WANCOURT at 6 am 21st
[illegible] [illegible] [illegible] [illegible] at
same time AAA Heavy and Div Arty
bombarding till [illegible] commencing [illegible]
6.30 am AAA [illegible] [illegible]
[illegible] [illegible] [illegible] about N32c 6.4
AAA after capture of [illegible] objectives [illegible]
along 14th 30th 21st Div [illegible]
[illegible] [illegible] [illegible] [illegible] prepared for
further advance East AAA 56 Div will
be prepared to follow in [illegible] [illegible] AAA
NVB will clear TIGRIS SWITCH trench as far
as WANCOURT line AAA it will [illegible]
NEPAL Trench between [illegible] [illegible] [illegible]
14th Div commencing 5.30 am and [illegible]
this [illegible] as soon after as possible AAA

From 56 Divn
Place
Time 12.45 am

The above may be forwarded as now corrected. (Z)

Censor. Signature of Addressor or person authorised to telegraph in his name.

* This line should be erased if not required.

100,000 Pads. W. 12093. M1217. McC. & Co., Ltd. 1/17. **(E. 764).** Forms C/2121/11.

"A" Form.
MESSAGES AND SIGNALS.

Army Form C. 2121

TO { 167 Inf Bde
    168 -
    169 -

Sender's Number: G 650
Day of Month: 11/4

AAA

It is probable that you may be called upon to take over front of NUB today in which case the two batteries detached with NUB will come again under your order. AAA added KEB reptd NUB and LOB.

From: 56 Div
Place:
Time: 8.45 am

(Z) Pakenham

"A" Form.
MESSAGES AND SIGNALS.

Army Form C. 2121 (in pads of 100).

TO	167	CRA	30 Div
	168	Q	VII Corps
	169		1+ Div

Sender's Number.	Day of Month.	In reply to Number.	AAA
G 670	11/4		

KEB will relieve NUB tonight AAA arrangements to be made direct between Brigadiers AAA areas on relief are shown on attached sketch map AAA KEB HQ will be in BACK Trench about N 14 d 05 AAA addsd KEB NUB repld LOB CRA and Q

From KITTY
Place
Time 4.47 pm

"A" Form.
MESSAGES AND SIGNALS.

Army Form C. 2121 (in pads of 100).

Prefix....Code....m	Words	Charge	This message is on a/c of:	Recd. at....m
Office of Origin and Service Instructions.	Sent		....Service.	Date....
	At....m.			From....
	To....			
	By....		(Signature of " Franking Officer.")	By....

TO { KEB   30 DW
     14 Div CRA
     NUB   7th Cps

Sender's Number.	Day of Month.	In reply to Number.	AAA
G.			

ADELA reports machine gun nests about cross roads N 22 a 64 and about N 22 central AAA and is proposing to ask for tanks to mop them up AAA KEB now relieving NUB AAA KEB will consolidate its position on high ground N 21 d N 22 c (Hill 90) and occupy ███████ and establish trenches running from N 27 6 96 to about N 28 6 by ██████ towards N 22 c 53 and its junction with NEPAL Trench about N 22 a 03 paying special attention to the flank towards WARLENCOURT AAA as soon as state of weather permits patrols will be pushed into HENINEL to clear up situation there AAA when EDITH has crossed COJEUL river and occupied HINDENBURG LINE to sunken road in N 34 A and B

From			
Place			
Time			

The above may be forwarded as now corrected. (Z)

"A" Form.
MESSAGES AND SIGNALS.

Army Form C. 2121 (in pads of 100).

| Prefix .... Code .... m. | Words | Charge | This message is on a/c of: | Recd. at .... m. |
| Office of Origin and Service Instructions. | Sent At .... m. To .... By .... | | .... Service. (Signature of "Franking Officer.") | Date .... From .... By .... |

TO

| Sender's Number. | Day of Month. | In reply to Number. | **A A A** |

KEB will occupy the continuation of that road, South East [Dust] and N.E. East of HENINEL & Cemetery cross roads N 29 ± A thence road running N.W. towards N 22 central junction out posts on [L] high ground N 29 C to connect up with BARBARA in N 35 A AAA added KEB rptd 7th Corps EDITH BARBARA ADELA NUB CRA

From KITTY

Place

Time 9·15 pm

The above may be forwarded as now corrected. (Z)

"A" Form.
MESSAGES AND SIGNALS.

Army Form C. 2121 (in pads of 100).
No of Message ....

Prefix.........Code.........m | Words | Charge | This message is on a/c of: | Recd. at.........m
Office of Origin and Service Instructions. | | | |
| | Sent | ....Service. | Date..........
| At.........m. | | From..........
| To......... | |
| By......... | (Signature of "Franking Officer.") | By..........

TO { HQ ?? CRA
     HQ ??
     ??? ???

Sender's Number | Day of Month | In reply to Number | AAA
6 | 12/4 | | M

When BARBARA has reached ??? ??? ?? ?? ?? ?? ?? ??? you ??? ???????? on ?? that road ?????? from ????? ???? ?? ?? ?? ?? N.35.D and ?? ?? ??? ?? ?? on this ?? AAA your ?????? with ADELA on Green Line will be ?? took about N.29.d.30 AAA ?? Green Line may be consolidated AAA ???????? AAA ???? KER ??? ??? ??? LOB and CRA

orders

From KITTY
Place
Time 11 A m

The above may be forwarded as now corrected. (Z)
Censor.   Signature of Addressor or person authorised to telegraph in his name.
* This line should be erased if not required.

"A" Form.
MESSAGES AND SIGNALS.

Army Form C. 2121 (in pads of 100).

TO: 169 Bde / 14 DW / 21st Div

N/

Sender's Number	Day of Month	In reply to Number	AAA
G.707	12/4		

As soon as ~~ADELA~~ is up in line on your left and ~~Div~~ BARBARA on your right you will send patrols forward toward the SENSEE river AAA These will be supported by formed bodies AAA usual touch to be kept laterally and communication maintained from front to rear by visual signalling AAA There will be no general advance from the Green line without orders from Div HQ AAA acknowledge AAA addd ZP1 reptd ADELA and BARBARA

From: KITTY
Place:
Time: 12.30 pm

(Z) Pakenham Lt Col

"A" Form.
MESSAGES AND SIGNALS.

Army Form C. 2121
(in pads of 100).

No of Message ....

Prefix .... Code .... m. | Words | Charge | This message is on a/c of: | Recd. at .... m.
Office of Origin and Service Instructions. | Sent | | Copy | Date ....
 | At .... m. | | Service. | From ....
 | To .... | | PRIORITY to | By ....
 | By .... | | (Signature of "Franking Officer.") 165th / 167th |

TO: 167th Inf. Bde.
188th Inf. Bde.   C.R.A.   A.D.M.S.   14th, 50th
189th Inf. Bde.   C.R.E.   Div.M.G.Offcr. 30th &
                                              61st Div.
AAA

Sender's Number: G.712   Day of Month: 12th

KSB will move to-day to vicinity of MERINAL, their H.Q. at N.14.d.0.4. being taken over by LOB AAA KSB will not have troops N. of the line of the NEUVILLE VITASSE — VANCOURT Road or W. of NEUVILLE VITASSE Trench AAA LOB will move up its rear battalion to N.14.c. & N. of road mentioned above AAA Such batteries as can be moved forward will be under command of Colonel McDOWELL and will come under orders of KSB AAA Orders re affiliation of R.E. etc follow AAA All units to be ready to move at short notice AAA ACKNOWLEDGE AAA Addressed 167th 188th & 189th Brigades C.R.A. C.R.E. "Q" A.D.M.S. Div. M.G.Officer Repeated VII Corps 14th, 50th, 30th and 61st Divisions

From: 56th Divn.
Place:
Time: 4-30 pm

The above may be forwarded as now corrected.   (Z)

Censor.   Signature of Addresser or person authorised to telegraph in his name.

"A" Form.
MESSAGES AND SIGNALS.

Army Form C. 2121
(in pads of 100).

| TO | 167 168 169 | Bdes | CRA CRE Ø | ADMS DwngOff VII Corps | 14 30 50 21 | Div | P |

Sender's Number: S 723
Day of Month: 12

GREEN line will be consolidated tonight as originally ordered and strong patrols sent forward towards the SENSEE river aaa 14 Dw have been ordered to make good the ridge in N24d today to enable VI Corps to enter GUEMAPPE aaa 50 Div will relieve 14 Div tonight aaa 21 Dw will continue to work down to COJEUL with aaa all preparations will be made to advance from the GREEN line to the line this SENSEE river tomorrow morning aaa

"A" Form.
MESSAGES AND SIGNALS.

Army Form C. 2121
(in pads of 100).

TO: 167/ 186/ Bde 169/

Attack by 5th Army will be renewed BULLECOURT front tomorrow and 6th Corps will advance simultaneously with 7th Corps aaa Reference my G.712 troops in will be held in readiness for forward move as tomorrow morning and but as therein ordered aaa added all recipients of G712

From 56 Div
Time 6.30 pm

"A" Form.
MESSAGES AND SIGNALS.

Army Form C. 2121 (in pads of 100).

Prefix	Code	m.	Words	Charge	This message is on a/c of:	Recd. at .... m.
Office of Origin and Service Instructions.			Sent At ... 6 .. m. To By		.... Service. (Signature of "Franking Officer.")	Date .... From .... By

TO { 169 Bde   50 Div
       VII Corps 21 Div

Sender's Number.	Day of Month.	In reply to Number.	AAA
S 737	13		

21 Div is continuing its advance at 9.55 am today aaa 169 Bde will conform to the advance of the Div along the 21st switch line in event of the 50 Div advance being the held up whilst 21 Div is to conform progress its movement its its secure flank that refusing its any Div is towards can early up necessary arrangements are if

From
Place
Time

The above may be forwarded as now corrected. **(Z)**

"A" Form.
MESSAGES AND SIGNALS.

Army Form C. 2121
(in pads of 100).

Have as before they advance place to log its 21st Div will they inform availed moves aaa bde addressed 16th Bde repeated VII Corps 50th and 21st Div

From 56 Div
Time 8.50

"A" Form.
MESSAGES AND SIGNALS.

Army Form C. 2121 (in pads of 100).

Prefix	Code	Words	Charge	This message is on a/c of:	Recd. at ... m.
Office of Origin and Service Instructions.		Sent		Copy	Date
		At ... m.		Service.	From
		To			
		By		(Signature of "Franking Officer.")	By

TO 178/Bde
    119/

Sender's Number.	Day of Month.	In reply to Number.	AAA
S 738	13		

The advance will continue at 9.55am today as listed in 56 Div follows between SENSEE area KEB and COJEUL river and LoG NEUVIS VITASSE COJEUL B COJEUL river and WANCOURT Line area NOB will in between to present area have that vacated by LoG was LoG will Accrindale GROPI in its area Movements not these area will the place were receipt of into from us 56 Div that advance has progressed successfully

From 56 Div
Place ---
Time   ---

The above may be forwarded as now corrected.   (Z)   [signature]

Censor.   Signature of Addresser or person authorised to telegraph in his name.
* This line should be erased if not required.

"A" Form.
MESSAGES AND SIGNALS.

Army Form C. 2121 (in pads of 100).

Prefix......Code......m.	Words	Charge	This message is on a/c of:	Recd. at ......m.
Office of Origin and Service Instructions.				Date......
	Sent		......Service.	From......
Priority for 169, 168	At......m. To...... By......		(Signature of "Franking Officer.")	By......

TO	167 Bde.	CRA		R
	168 "			
	169 "			

| Sender's Number. | Day of Month. | In reply to Number. | AAA |
| * g 758 | 13/4 | | |

Warning Order AAA Corps will attack tomorrow and gain line SENSEE River AAA Right boundary of 56 Div N.35 a 97 - road junction O 31 c 36 - N. edge of wood U 2 A (wood exclusive) AAA left boundary WANCOURT TOWER - O 25 b 55 - CHERISY (village inclusive) AAA 1st Objective road junction O 31 c 36 - along road track through O 31 a & b - O 25 d 60 thence North to O 25 b 55 AAA 2nd Objective Sunken road from N. corner of wood in U 2 A - CHERISY village inclusive AAA creeping barrage one hundred yards in four minutes details follow AAA. KEB will carry out attack AAA LOB and NVB will probably not be required to move AAA Zero hour will be

From
Place
Time

The above may be forwarded as now corrected. (Z)
...... Censor. Signature of Addresser or person authorised to telegraph in his name.
* This line should be erased if not required.

"A" Form.
MESSAGES AND SIGNALS.

Army Form C. 2121 (in pads of 100).

No of Message..........

Prefix......Code......m.	Words	Charge	This message is on a/c of:	Recd. at ......m.
Office of Origin and Service Instructions.	Sent		............Service.	Date............
	At..........m.			From............
	To..........		(Signature of "Franking Officer.")	By............
	By..........			

TO {

Sender's Number.	Day of Month.	In reply to Number.	**A A A**

march late AAA probably early AAA
units on flanks also taking part AAA
acknowledge AAA also KRA LOB
NUB and CRA

From: KITTY
Place:
Time: 6.40 pm

The above may be forwarded as now corrected. (Z) Blakenham Lt Col

Censor. Signature of Addresser or person authorised to telegraph in his name.

Copy

"A" Form.
MESSAGES AND SIGNALS.

Army Form C. 2121
(in pads of 100).

Prefix... Code... m.	Words	Charge	This message is on a/c of:	Recd. at ... m.
Office of Origin and Service Instructions.	Sent		...Service.	Date...
	At... m.			From...
	To			
	By		(Signature of "Franking Officer.")	By

TO — 169 Bde

Sender's Number.	Day of Month.	In reply to Number.	A A A
G 769	14/4		

Owing to plans of 29th Div not fitting in with those of 50th Div the 151 Bde will be moving forward on your left and will be forming a defensive flank across spurs in O.19 O.20 O.26. roughly along railway in those squares

From 56 Div
Place
Time 6.20 a.m.

Blakeway Lt

"A" Form.
MESSAGES AND SIGNALS.

Office of Origin and Service Instructions:
Copy

TO: 168 Bde
     169 Bde

Sender's Number: G.772
Day of Month: 14

Move two Battalions forward into COJEUL SWITCH line between NEUVILLE VITASSE — WANCOURT Road and to WANCOURT line aaa KEB forward officers to HQ from those Battalions aaa for liason aaa Battalions remain under your orders aaa until further orders aaa Cojeul ridge now addressed LOB reported KEB

From: 56 Div
Time:

MESSAGES AND SIGNALS.

Priority

TO: 169 Brigade
168 Brigade

Sender's Number: G 779
Day of Month: 14*

AAA

In continuation G772 aaa Leading Battalion 168 Brigade is placed at your disposal aaa Cockcroft This is LOSK and HQ and is The EGG N 20 D aaa actuality AAA added 169 and 168 Bdes.

From: 58 Division
Time: 11.22 AM.

"A" Form.
MESSAGES AND SIGNALS.

Army Form C. 2121 (in pads of 100).

TO: 21st Div
169 Bde

Sender's Number: G.780
Day of Month: 14/4

AAA

21st Div have reported strong German counter attack developing from NE and have ordered the trench block in T5a to N34B81 and the strong points in that area to be strongly held and have arranged to reinforce HINDENBURG line between N.34.B.81 and N.28.D.20 at very short notice AAA should this attack develop you in the way expected you should arrange to attack it in flank AAA meanwhile arrange to secure HENINEL strongly AAA addrd 169 Bde repld 21st Div

From: 56 Div
Place:
Time: 11.57 am

(Z) B Pakenham Wlyh

"A" Form.
MESSAGES AND SIGNALS.
Army Form C. 2121 (in pads of 100).

Prefix .... Code .... m.	Words	Charge	This message is on a/c of:	Recd. at .... m.
Office of Origin and Service Instructions.	Sent		.... Service.	Date ....
	At .... m.			From ....
	To			
	By		(Signature of " Franking Officer.")	By ....

TO { 167 Bde, 168 Bde, 169 Bde } CRA

Sender's Number.	Day of Month.	In reply to Number.	
* G.783	14/16		AAA

Following for ~~the~~ in view of the Corps general advance aaa situation on the Corps to be adjusted on the line will be gained made Corps not be pressed aaa and be ground ends aaa Acknowledge Addressed 3 Brigades and CRA.

From 56 Division
Place
Time 1.5 pm

"A" Form.
MESSAGES AND SIGNALS.

Army Form C. 2121
(in pads of 100).

TO { 168 Bde 50th Div
     169 Bde
     21st Div }

Sender's Number: G.784
Day of Month: 14/4

KEB has ordered LOSK to occupy at once the trenches East and South of Hill 90 in N.22.c and N.28.a with HQ at the COT AAA LOB will dispose his troops so as to be able to occupy COJEUL SWITCH northward from the WANCOURT LINE to map square 14 facing WANCOURT at very short notice AAA This in view of reported impending counter attack by Germans on GUEMAPPE AAA addsd LOB repld KEB BARBARA and ENID

From: KITTY
Time: 1.12 pm

"A" Form.
MESSAGES AND SIGNALS.

Army Form C. 2121 (in pads of 100).

TO:
- 167 Bde — CRA — 2nd Dvr Tp
- 168 — Q — 3rd Dvr
- 169 — CRE — 5th Dvr

Sender's Number: G788
Day of Month: 14/4
AAA

KEB will be relieved tonight by LOB AAA relief to be complete by 4 am tomorrow AAA KEB on relief to proceed to area at present occupied by LOB AAA Tomorrow KEB may exchange the open exchange area with NUB. AAA present HQ's to be exchanged AAA Details to be settled by Brigadiers AAA acknowledge AAA addr KEB LOB NUB reply CRA CRE Q

From: KITTY
Place:
Time: 3.30 pm

Blakenham Lt Col

"A" Form.
MESSAGES AND SIGNALS.

Army Form C.2121.
(In pads of 100.)

Prefix... Code... in Words.	Charge.	This message is on a/c of:	Recd. at .... m.
Office of Origin and Service Instructions.	Sent At .... m.	.... Service.	Date ......
Priority	To .... By	(Signature of "Franking Officer.")	From ...... By ......

TO { 168 Bde
     167
     169

Sender's Number.	Day of Month.	In reply to Number.	AAA
G 800	14/4		

The leading Bde will continue to sieze every opportunity of making ground to the front with the object of reaching by by the night April 16th a line as near as possible to the second objective described in Div Op Order 82 of 13th inst 9th AAA Leading troops must use hours of darkness to push forward machine guns and establish posts along high ground AAA Boundaries remain unchanged AAA for any operation for which Tanks desired 8 hours notice required at Div HQ AAA following defensive lines will be consolidated AAA second line N.35.A ~~M.29.d.0.~~ AAA forward line T.5 N.21.D N.16.C central AAA Acknowledge AAA adddd 3 Inf Bdes

From KITTY
Place
Time 10.20 pm

The above may be forwarded as now corrected. (Z)

Censor.   Signature of Addresser or person authorised to telegraph in his name.
* This line should be erased if not required.

"A" Form.
MESSAGES AND SIGNALS.
Army Form C. 2121 (in pads of 100).
No of Message ....

Prefix....Code......m	Words	Charge	This message is on a/c of:	Recd. at ......m.
Office of Origin and Service Instructions				Date..........
	Sent		Service.	
	At........m.			From........
	To........		(Signature of "Franking Officer.")	By........
	By........			

TO { 168 Bde
    167 "
    169 "

| Sender's Number. | Day of Month. | In reply to Number. | |
| G 829 | 15/4 | | AAA |

refce my G 800 of 14th AAA This
is now modified as regards
the scope of the progress to be made
AAA it will suffice if the leading
Divs can work forward to the
approx line T6 central O 31 C
O 19 central in next three days
AAA essential to consolidate all
ground gained AAA addd LOB
reptd NUB and KEB

From KITTY
Place
Time 9 5 pm

The above may be forwarded as now corrected. (Z) Blakeney Lt Col
Censor. Signature of Addressor or person authorised to telegraph in his name.

"A" Form.
MESSAGES AND SIGNALS.

Army Form C. 2121 (in pads of 100)

Prefix...Code...m	Words	Charge	This message is on a/c of:	Recd. at ...m.
Office of Origin and Service Instructions.	Sent		...Service.	Date...
Priority 80	At ...m. To... By...		Copy (Signature of Franking Officer.)	From... By...

TO: 167 Brigade
    168 Brigade   AA

Sender's Number.	Day of Month.	In reply to Number.	AAA
G845 Priority	16		

One Battalion 167 Brigade is placed at disposal of 168 Brigade and will proceed to Hill 90 on receipt of this order and an Officer will be sent to report to Headquarters 168 Brigade forthwith aaa Acknowledge aaa addressed 167 Brigade repeated 168 Brigade

From: 56 Division
Place:
Time: 9.6 pm.

"A" Form.
MESSAGES AND SIGNALS.

Army Form C. 2121
(in pads of 100).

No. of Message ....

Prefix ...... Code ...... m. | Words | Charge | This message is on a/c of: | Recd. at ...... m.
Office of Origin and Service Instructions. | Sent | | | Date
Copy | At ...... m. | | .... Service. | From BB
| To | | | By
| By | | (Signature of "Franking Officer.") |

TO: BGB-167 Bde 168 Bde 169 Bde
    VII Corps   VII Corps HA   33 DW
                                  56 DW

Sender's Number: G 874
Day of Month: 18
In reply to Number:
AAA

Information from battle towers are battalions of Bde 167 Bde Corps 56 Div. attacked battalion at Bde 33 VII Div. German attack 1pm near disposed once septd 56 Corps. prisoners on today Place of aaa 168 Div HA. posts W IN COURT by one 168 added 169 VII CRA.

From: 56 DW
Place:
Time: 11 am

The above may be forwarded as now corrected. (Z)

Censor. Signature of Addressor or person authorised to telegraph in his name

App. II

SECRET. 56th Division G.A.117.

56th DIVISION INSTRUCTIONS

DRESS & EQUIPMENT.

Dress & Equipment will be as laid down in the pamphlet "Training of Divisions for Offensive Action" (S.S.135) para XXXI, pages 58 & 59, with the following exceptions :-

(a) The greatcoat will not be worn, but will be dumped in accordance with Orders issued by 56th Division "Q".

The leather jerkin may be worn.

(b) At least one aeroplane flare will be carried by all ranks.

(c) Two sandbags instead of three will be carried.

(d) Picks and Shovels. One heavy tool per man or as far as the supply admits.

The C.R.E. will arrange to meet the requirements of the three Brigades as far as possible.

(e) Artillery flags coloured yellow with a black cross, will be issued by 56th Division "Q".

Units are reminded that these flags must not be stuck in the ground, and will mean nothing unless they are waved (see S.S.135, p.15.).

(f) Stokes Shells, specially prepared may be carried by Mopping up Parties in place of "P" Grenades for dealing with dugouts.

B. Pakenham
Lieut-Colonel,
General Staff.

Head Qrs. 56th Divn.
1st April, 1917.

Copies to -
167th Infantry Brigade.	A. P. M.
168th Infantry Brigade.	193rd Div.M.G.Coy. A.D.M.S.
169th Infantry Brigade.	56th Div. Signals. "Q"
VII Corps.	" " Train. File.
" " Artillery.	Div. M.G.Officer.
" " Heavy Artillery.	Div. Gas Officer.
" " M.G.Officer.	D.A.D.O.S.
14th Division.	4th Aust.Div.Supply Column.
30th Division.	No.2 Ammn.Sub Park.
C.R.A. C.R.E. 1/5th Ches Rt.	G.O.C. A.D.C. War Diary

SECRET.   56th Divn. No.G.A.185.

56th DIVISION INSTRUCTIONS.

T A N K S.

1. Sixteen Tanks of "D" Battalion, 1st Brigade, Heavy Branch M.G.Corps will work with the VII Corps.

    Headquarters 1st Brigade, Heavy Branch M.G.Corps will be at MONTENESCOURT.

    Headquarters "D" Battalion will be in ARRAS about G.21.a. (CONVENT de NOTRE DAME).

2. 1 Section (4 Tanks) will be allotted to the 56th Division.

3. Each half Section (2 Tanks) will be accompanied by 1 Section of Infantry to assist them in their advance where required.   These Sections will be furnished by 169th Infantry Brigade.

4. These two Sections of Infantry will no longer be required once the BLUE LINE has been reached.

5. The 2 Section Commanders will meet Lieut. BELL (O.C.Section of Tanks working with the Division) at Divisional Headquarters at 10.45 a.m. on April 4th.

6. The two Infantry Sections will undergo a preliminary training with the Heavy Branch Machine Gun Company.
    Details re attachment will be notified later.

7. The C.R.E. will detail an Officer to meet Lieut.BELL at 11 a.m. on 4th April at Divisional Headquarters, and will be prepared to attach this Officer and 3 R.E. N.C.Os. to "D" Battalion, should their services be required.

8. A Map is attached shewing approximately the Tank objectives and direction of routes to them.

    Continuous GREEN Lines show lines of advance to 1st objective.
    Dotted GREEN lines show lines of advance to 2nd objective.

9. After the capture of the BLUE LINE the Tanks will act in accordance with the orders issued to them   direct by VII Corps.

10. If Zero is at dawn, Tanks will be able to move up during Z - 1/Z night to points as close up to our Front Line as is consistent with the safety of the Infantry.

11. Tanks will move on to the BLUE LINE following up the leading infantry and will not proceed any great distance in front of them, otherwise the Infantry will not be in a position to take advantage of the opportunities that the Tanks may create.

12. ACKNOWLEDGE.

                                                B Pakenham
                                                Lieut-Colonel,
                                                General Staff.
Head Qrs. 56th Divn.
2nd April, 1917.

                    P.T.O.

Copies to -
167th Infantry Brigade.
168th Infantry Brigade.
169th Infantry Brigade.
VII Corps.
" "   Artillery.
" "   Heavy Artillery.
" "   M.G.Officer.
14th Division.
30th Division.
C.R.A.
C.R.E.
1/5th Cheshire Regt.
A.P.M.
193rd Div. M.G.Coy.
56th Div. Signals.
1st Bde. H.B. M.G.Corps.
"D" Battalion " " "
Lieut.BELL c/o "D" Battalion

56th Div. Train.
Div. M.G.Officer.
Div. Gas Officer.
D.A.D.O.S.
4th Aust.Div.Supply Column.
No.2 Ammn. Sub Park.
G.O.C.
A.D.C.
A.D.M.S.
"Q"
War Diary
File.

SECRET.   56th Divn. No.G.A.97.

56th DIVISION INSTRUCTIONS.

Signal Communication.

1. The methods of communication will be as follows :-

    1. Telephone and Telegraph.
    2. Visual.
    3. Pigeons.
    4. Power Buzzer.
    5. Contact Aeroplanes.
    6. Despatch Riders.
    7. Wireless.

2. Advanced Divisional Head Qrs. (M.3.c.50.10.) will be in direct telephonic communication with :-

    1. VII Corps (also Telegraph)
    2. 14th Division. (WALRUS)
    3. 30th Division (Advanced Head Qrs. at BLAIRVILLE QUARRY)
    4. 167th Infantry Brigade (M.10.d.20.25.)
    5. 168th Infantry Brigade (M.10.d.9.9.)
    6. 169th Infantry Brigade (M.3.b.35.95.)

    The C.R.A. will be in direct telephonic communication with :-

    G.O.C. R.A. VII Corps.
    Headquarters VII Corps Heavy Artillery (BERNEVILLE)
    280th R.F.A.Bde. Group (M.16.a.60.67.)
    281st R.F.A.Bde. Group (M.3.d.5.0.)
    251st R.F.A.Bde. Group (M.3.c.45.20.)
    250th R.F.A.Bde. Group (M.8.b.4.2.)
    293rd R.F.A.Bde. Group (M.3.c.45.30.)

3. The Advanced Divisional Exchange will be at M.3.c.50.10.

4. A Liaison Exchange will be established at M.3.c.50.10. to which will be connected all Infantry Brigades & Artillery Groups only.

5. A special issue of 12 miles of cable will be made to each assaulting Infantry Brigade, for lines across NO MAN'S LAND.

6. The assaulting Brigades will be connected by direct lines, with the Flanking Brigades.

    <u>167th Infantry Brigade</u> with the Left Brigade of the 30th Division in Railway Cutting at S.3.a.7.2.

    <u>168th Infantry Brigade</u> with the Right Brigade of the 14th Division - KETSAS STREET G.34.d.8.8.

7. Visual Signal Stations will be established as follows :-

    (1) M.3.c.50.20.) For communication between
    (2) M.10.d.70.25.) Adv. Div. H.Qrs. and the
) Assaulting Brigades.
    (3) M.11.c.20.20 for communication between the Assaulting Brigade H. Qrs. and Assaulting Battalions.

/The

- 2 -

The personnel for Station (1) will be found by 169th Infantry Brigade, Stations (2) and (3) will be connected by telephone with 167th and 168th Brigade Headquarters.

The personnel for No. (2) and (3) Stations will be found by 168th and 167th Brigades respectively.

8. PIGEONS. Up to and including Z day 8 pigeons will be supplied to each Infantry Brigade for distribution to Battalions.

9. The Division has 4 Power Buzzer Sets allotted as follows :-

167th Brigade 3 Power Buzzers 2 Amplifiers
168th Brigade 1 Power Buzzer only.

Personnel will be supplied by Battalion Signallers who have been trained in the use of Power Buzzers.

Extra Carriers will be required on the scale of 2 per Amplifier. (see attached sketch).

10. Station Calls will be allotted later.

11. WIRELESS. The Division has two Wireless Sets. One will be allotted to 168th Infantry Brigade at disposal of Brigade Commander. The Second Set will be established at ~~Advd. Divisional Headquarters at M.3.c.5.0.~~ M10.6.6.7.
The Corps directing station will be at 51B.G.32.c.2.1
Operators will be supplied by Corps Signal Coy.
4 extra carriers will be required for Set in forward area and should be detailed from men who attended course of instruction at LA GORGUE.
The dug-out at about M.24.b.50.15. is now reserved for the set allotted to 168th Infantry Brigade.

B Pakenham

Head Qrs. 56th Divn.
4th April, 1917.

Lieut-Colonel,
General Staff.

Copies to :-
167th Infantry Brigade.
168th Infantry Brigade.
169th Infantry Brigade.
VII Corps.
 "   "   Artillery.
 "   "   Heavy Artillery.
 "   "   M.G.Officer.
14th Division.
30th Division.
C.R.A.
C.R.E.
1/5th Cheshire Regt.
A.P.M.
193rd Div. M.G.Coy.
56th Div. Signals.

56th Div. Train.
Div. M.G.Officer.
Div. Gas Officer.
D.A.D.O.S.
4th Aust. Div. Supply Column.
No. 2 Ammn. Sub Park.
G.O.C.
A.D.C.
A.D.M.S.
"Q"
War Diary.
File.

No 8 Squad R?C

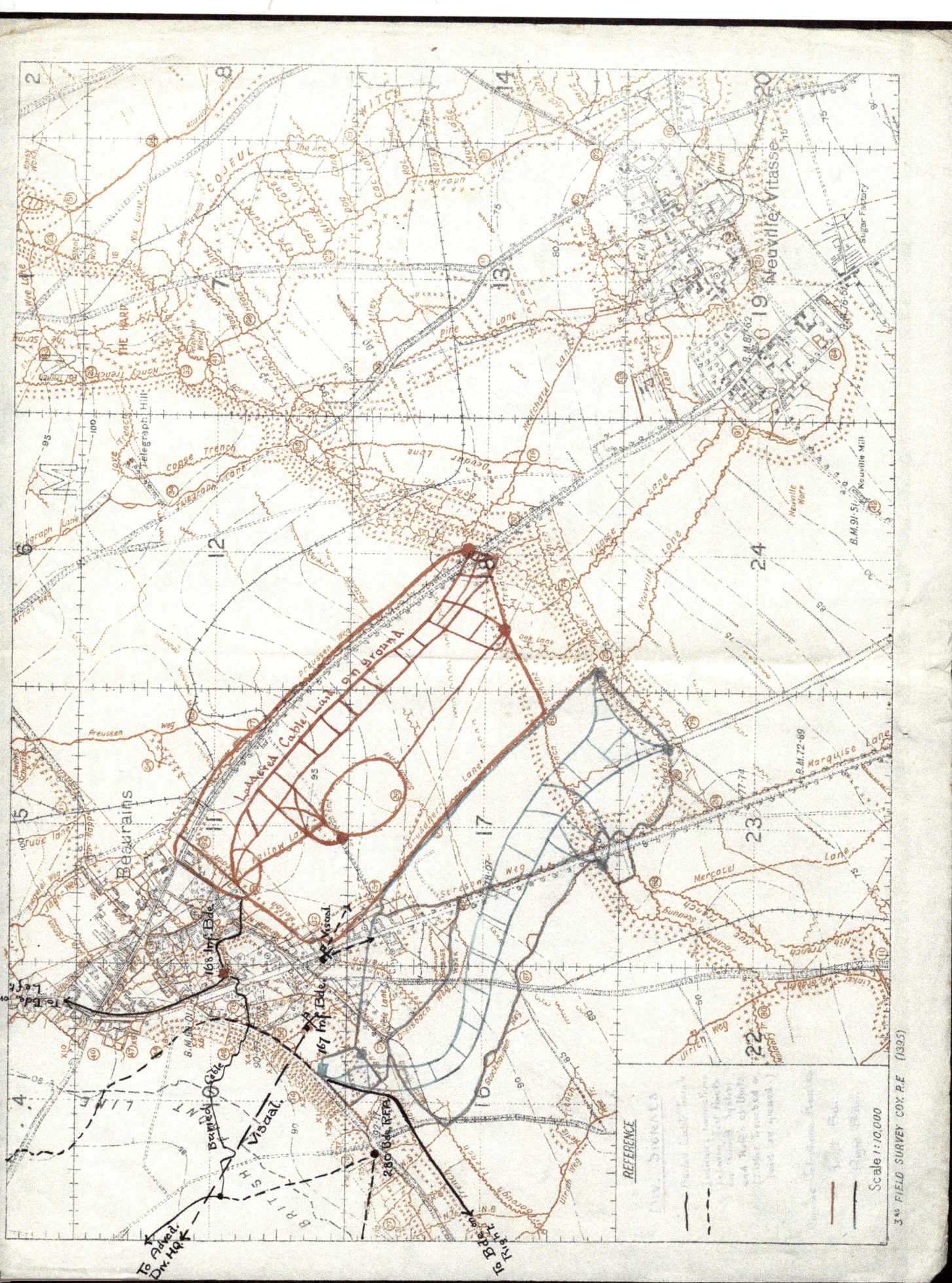

1st PHASE

P.B. for sending
A for receiving

For second phase remains in same position and acts as transmitting station for No.3 P.B.

Moving forward with Batt'n Hqrs →

No 2.A — to receive acknowledgements of back station

No 2.P.B — For sending to Back Station

No.3.PB — Held in reserve to replace possible casualties and for use in Second Phase

No 1 PB — Back Station

No 1.A

167th FRONT

No 4.PB

← Moving forward with Batt'n Hqrs

168th FRONT

SECRET. 56th Divn. No. G.A.168.

56th DIVISION INSTRUCTIONS.

FLAGS.

The following Signals will be used to mark the advance of the leading Infantry :-

    <u>21st Div.</u>   NIL.

    <u>30th Div.</u>   (1). RED & YELLOW FLAGS. These flags have no meaning unless waved.

        (2). Tin Discs to be worn on the backs of troops of assaulting battalions

    <u>56th Div.</u>   YELLOW FLAGS with BLACK ST.GEORGE'S CROSS. These flags have no meaning unless waved.

    <u>14th Div.</u>   Artillery Boards, top half RED, lower half YELLOW.

The 14th Division will also put up WHITE BOARDS with BLACK DIAGONAL CROSS at CROSS ROAD, etc. as reference boards for Artillery.

ACKNOWLEDGE, please.

Head Qrs. 56th Divn.
4th April, 1917.

                              Lieut-Colonel,
                              General Staff.

Copies to -

167th Infantry Brigade.	56th Div. Train.
168th Infantry Brigade.	Div. M.G.Officer.
168th Infantry Brigade.	Div. Gas Officer.
14th Division.	D.A.D.O.S.
30th Division.	4th Aust.Div.Supply Column.
21st Division.	No. 2 Ammn. Sub Park.
C.R.A.	A.D.V.S.
C.R.E.	No. 8 Squadron R.F.C.
1/5th Cheshire Regt.	G.O.C.
A.P.M.	A.D.C.
193rd Div.M.G.Coy.	A.D.M.S.
56th Div.Signals.	"Q"
	War Diary.
	File.

War Diary

SECRET.   56th Div.No.G.A.172.

56th DIVISION INSTRUCTIONS.

TANKS (No.2).

In continuation of previous instructions dated 2nd April, the procedure to be adopted by the Tanks allotted to 56th Divn. after the capture of the BLUE LINE will be as follows :-

They will proceed to a Tank Refilling Point about M.18.d.6.3. at which place the O.C. Right Assaulting Battalion of the 168th Infantry Brigade will get into touch with the Tank Section Commander, and arrange to keep him informed as to the situation, so that he may be able to decide on the best method of carrying out the further task allotted to him by higher authority on the advance from the BLUE LINE taking place.

B Pakenham

Head Qrs. 56th Divn.   Lieut-Colonel,

4th April, 1917.   General Staff.

Copies to -

    167th Infantry Brigade.   56th Div. Train.
    168th Infantry Brigade.   Div. M.G.Officer.
    169th Infantry Brigade.   Div. Gas Officer.
    VII Corps.   D.A.D.O.S.
    "   "   Artillery.   4th Aust. Div.Supply Column.
    "   "   Heavy Artillery.   No. 2 Ammn. Sub Park.
    "   "   M.G.Officer.   G.O.C.
    14th Division.   A.D.C.
    30th Division.   A.D.M.S.
    C.R.A.   "Q"
    C.R.E.   War Diary.
    1/5th Cheshire Regt.   File.
    A.P.M.
    193rd Div. M.G.Coy.
    56th Div. Signals.
    1st Bde. H.B. M.G.Corps.
    "D" Battalion "   "   "
    Lieut.BELL c/o "D" Bn.

SECRET. 56th Div.No.G.A.173.

56th DIVISION INSTRUCTIONS.

CONTACT AEROPLANE SIGNALLING INSTRUCTIONS.

1. An aeroplane for contact patrol work will be allotted from No. 8 Squadron R.F.C. This aeroplane will be distinguished by a black band under the right hand plane, with a blue extension streamer.

2. One aeroplane ground flare will be carried by each man.

   The ground flare will be lit placed at the bottom of trenches, shell holes or behind ruins, banks or other cover, by the furthest forward troops only, when called for by contact aeroplane. The signal from the aeroplane to light flares will be either by Klaxon horn, i.e. a succession of A's or by firing White Very Lights.

3. The approximate times at which flares will be lit will be notified in final Operation Orders.

   The flares used by the Infantry will be RED.

   Cavalry will use GREEN FLARES.

3. Signals from troops to an aeroplane will be by White ground strips pinned to the ground forming the code letter or letters required, the tops of the letters pointing towards the enemy. Each letter should not be less than 4' x 4'.

   The following letters will be used :-

B's	Enemy are retiring at
F's	Enemy offering strong resistance at
G's	Further bombardment required.
H's	Lengthen range.
J's	Raise barrage.
K's	Lower barrage.
O's	Barrage wanted
P's	Reinforcements wanted.
N's	Short of ammunition.
W's	Short of water.
Y's	Short of grenades.
X's	Held up by M.G.fire.
Z's	Held up by wire.
O.K.	We are all right.

/The

- 2 -

The aeroplane will acknowledge these signals by sending a series of T's on the Klaxon Horn and will mark on a map where seen and drop it at Corps Dropping Station at R.12.d.3.9.

The ground strips must be removed the moment the signal has been acknowledged by the aeroplane. A written or telegraphic message must be sent in addition.

4. Brigade H.Q. will not lay out their three quarter circle ground sheets and letters but will use their Signalling Panels for sending messages.

5. Instructions for Contact Patrol Work by Aeroplanes, Appendix "B" S.S.135 will be followed except as laid down above.

B Pakenham

Lieut-Colonel,
General Staff.

Head Qrs. 56th Divn.
4th April, 1917.

Copies to -

167th Infantry Brigade.
168th Infantry Brigade.
169th Infantry Brigade.
VII Corps
" " Artillery.
" " Heavy Artillery.
" " M.G.Officer.
14th Division.
30th Division.
U.R.A.
C.R.E.
1/5th Cheshire Regt.
A.P.M.
193rd Div. M.G.Coy.
56th Div. Signals.
1st Bde. H.B. M.G.Corps.
"D" Bn. " " "
Lieut.BELL c/o "D" Bn.

No. 8 Squadron R.F.C.
56th Div. Train.
Div. M.G.Officer.
Div. Gas Officer.
D.A.D.O.S.
4th Aust. Div. Supply Column.
No. 2 Ammn. Sub Park.
G.C.C.
A.D.C.
A.D.M.S.
"Q"
War Diary.
File.

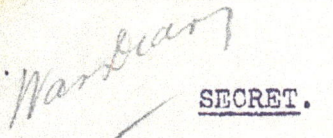

SECRET. 56th Div.No.G.A.177.

56th DIVISION INSTRUCTIONS.

CONCENTRATION AND ASSEMBLY.

1. 56th Division No. G.A.105 is cancelled and the following substituted.

2. On "W" & "X" days at 10 a.m. the disposition of troops will be as under :-

    167th & 168th Brigades in the Line.
    169th Brigade in Reserve (Brigade Headquarters
                at   (3 Battalions.
          MONCHIET.(169th T.M.Bty.
                    2 Sections 193rd M.G.Coy.

    at BEAUMETZ   1 Battalion.

    at ACHICOURT   169th M.G.Coy. & 193rd M.G.Coy.
                                (less 2 Sections

3. On X day and night X/Y the following moves will take place :-

    167th Brigade will move into AREA "A"
    168th Brigade will move into AREAS "B" & "C".

These moves will be completed by <u>6 p.m.</u> with the exception of the 1 Company 1/5th Cheshire Regiment, who will not join 168th Brigade till dark.

169th Brigade (less Brigade H.Qrs. & 1 Battalion at BEAUMETZ) will move into Area "C1" ACHICOURT & AGNY.

ROUTE.

    Main ARRAS - DOULLENS Rd. - L.35.b.5.8.

RESTRICTIONS.

    (a). An interval of 200 yards will be kept between Companies.
    (b). No troops may leave ARRAS before dark.

4. On "Y" day, the remaining Battalion, 169th Brigade will clear BEAUMETZ by 9 a.m. and relieve "A" Battalion, 168th Brigade in "C" Area at 6 p.m. 2 Sections 193rd M.G.Coy. will follow the above to Area detailed by G.O.C. 169th Inf.Bde.

5. Brigadier-General Commanding 169th Brigade, will, at 12 noon "Y" day take over Headquarters of 168th Brigade near

                                                          /ACHICOURT MILL.

ACHICOURT MILL. The Brigadier-General Commanding 168th Brigade moving at that hour to his Battle Headquarters in BEAURAINS.

6. On Y/Z night Brigades will take over their Assembly Areas.

A map showing Assembly Areas was forwarded under Divisional Instructions "Assembly Areas" No. G.A.96, dated 30th March.

B Pakenham,
Lieut-Colonel,
General Staff.

Head Qrs. 56th Divn.
4th April, 1917.

Copies to :-

167th Infantry Brigade.
168th Infantry Brigade.
169th Infantry Brigade.
VII Corps.
" " Artillery.
" " Heavy Artillery.
" " M.G.Officer.
14th Division.
30th Division.
C.R.A.
C.R.E.
1/5th Cheshire Regt.
A.P.M.
193rd Div. M.G.Coy.

56th Div. Signals.
56th Div. Train.
No. 8 Squadron R.F.C.
Div. M.G.Officer.
Div. Gas Officer.
D.A.D.O.S.
4th Aust.Div.Supply Column.
No. 2 Ammn. Sub Park.
G.O.C.
A.D.C.
A.D.M.S.
"Q"
War Diary.
File.

SECRET.   56th Div.No.G.A.177

56th DIVISION INSTRUCTIONS.

SIGNAL INSTRUCTIONS NO.2 for CODE CALLS, Etc.

1. Code Calls for Division, Brigades & Battalions.

	Codes up to Zero.	After Zero.
Division.	YEF.	YEF.
167th Inf.Bde.	NUB.	ZPG.
7th Middlesex	CROWN	GMI
8th Middlesex	INK.	HMI.
1st Londons	MIT.	ALO.
3rd Londons	HOW.	CLO.
168th Inf.Bde.	LOP.	ZPH.
4th Londons.	WHEAT	DLO.
12th Londons	BAY.	LLO.
13th Londons	KEN.	MLO.
14th Londons	LOSK.	NLO.
169th Inf.Bde.	KEB.	ZPI.
2nd Londons.	ATTEN.	BLO.
5th Londons	BAT.	ELO.
9th Londons	DICK.	ILO.
16th Londons	SHOU.	PLO.

2. Wireless Station - Power Buzzer Calls.

Power Buzzer allotted to 168th Inf.Bde. will use the call CP.

167th Infantry Brigade. Power Buzzer established in Front Line will use the call CO.

Power Buzzer moving forward with Battalion Headquarters will use the call CN.

Power Buzzer held in Reserve for use in second phase will use the call CM.

3. No Wireless Messages will be sent in clear unless franked "in clear" and signed by a Staff Officer.

The "BAB" Trench Code or the Playfair Cipher (with the key word "CROSSMAN") will be used for messages sent by wireless and Power Buzzer.

4. Signalling between Infantry and Aircraft.

As laid down in S.S.135 "Instructions for Training of Divisions for Offensive Action" Appendix "B".

B Pakenham

Head Qrs. 56th Divn.   Lieut-Colonel,
4th April, 1917.   General Staff.

P.T.O.

56th Div.No.G.A.180.

Copies to -

- 167th Infantry Brigade.
- 168th Infantry Brigade
- 169th Infantry Brigade.
- VII Corps.
- "   "   Artillery.
- "   "   Heavy Artillery.
- "   "   M.G.Officer.
- 14th Division.
- 30th Division.
- C.R.A.
- C.R.E.
- 1/5th Cheshire Regt.
- A.P.M.
- 193rd Div.M.G.Coy.
- A.D. Signals, VIIth Corps.

- 56th Div. Signals.
- 56th Div. Train.
- No. 8 Squadron R.F.C.
- Div.M.G.Officer.
- Div.Gas Officer.
- D.A.D.O.S.
- 4th Aust.Div.Supply Column.
- No.2 Ammn.Sub Park.
- G.O.C.
- A.D.C.
- A.D.M.S.
- "Q"
- War Diary.
- File.

<u>SECRET.</u>   56th Divn.G.A.124/1

167th Infantry Brigade.	56th Div. Train.
168th Infantry Brigade	Div. M.G.Officer.
169th Infantry Brigade.	Div. Gas Officer.
C.R.A.	D.A.D.O.S.
C.R.E.	4th Aust. Biv.Supply Column.
1/5th Cheshire Regt.	No. 2 Ammn. Sub Park.
A.D.M.S.	G.O.C.
"Q"	A.D.C.
A.P.M.	War Diary.
193rd Div. M.G.Coy.	File.
56th Div. Signals.	

The time signal will be sent from Army Headquarters at 8 p.m. daily as well as at 9 a.m.

Div Sigs will repeat.

B Pakenham

Head Qrs. 56th Divn.
4th April, 1917.

Lieut-Colonel,
General Staff.

SECRET.

56th Divn.G.A.167.

167th Infantry Bde.	Div M.G. Officer.
168th Infantry Bde.	Div. Gas Officer.
169th Infantry Bde.	D.A.D.O.S.
C.R.A.	4th Aust. Div. Supply Column.
C.R.E. 1/5th Ches. Regt.	No. 2 Ammn. Sub Park.
A.P.M.	G.O.C.
193rd Div. M.G.Coy.	A.D.C.
56th Div. Signals.	A.D.M.S.
56th Div. Train.	"Q"
	War Diary.
	File.

On V, W, and X days the bombardment will begin on each day as soon as the light is good enough to permit of effective observation.

On Y day the hour the bombardment will begin will be notified.

B Pakenham
Lieut-Colonel,
General Staff.

Head Qrs. 56th Divn.
4th April, 1917.

SECRET.  56th Divn. G.A.221.

56TH DIVISION INSTRUCTIONS.

OPERATIONS.

I. (a). In the event of the Corps on the left not making good its first objective, VII Corps has stated that the 14th & 56th Divisions will not go forward to the attack on the BLUE LINE.

(b). Should this happen, it is hoped that sufficient notice will be received to allow of the necessary warning reaching all concerned by telegram or telephone, but the time may be so short that a visual signal is also necessary.
A flag pole will, therefore, be erected at Advanced Div. H.Q. on the Railway Embankment at N.3.b.5.1. and the signal for the cancelling of the attack will be the hoisting of the following flag :-

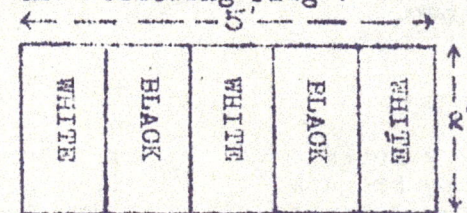

Flag poles will also be erected by Infantry Brigades as follows :-
    167th Infantry Brigade - M.17.a.07.
    168th Infantry Brigade

Flags will be supplied by O.C. Div. Signal Coy.

This signal will be carefully watched for from Infantry Brigade Advanced H.Q. and from Group H.Qrs., and all arrangements made to warn all concerned at once by similar flag signal as well as by telephone.

It should be noted, that, as the signal for the commencement of the barrage and for the infantry to advance is a simultaneous salvo by all Field Artillery, the fact that the barrage does not commence will in itself be a notification to the infantry that there is a postponement.

II. (a). Should the 14th Division fail to reach the BLUE LINE, VII Corps has stated that the 56th Division, if it has reached it, will halt on it and form a defensive left flank.

(b). In this event, in addition to warning by telephone, the following flag signal will be hoisted at Advanced Div. H.Q.

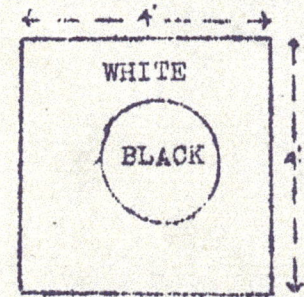

The same instructions apply as in para. I (a).

P.T.O. /III.

III. The flags for Div. H.Q. will be kept personally by the O.C. Signals, and will only be hoisted by the direct orders of an Officer of the General Staff.

O.C. Signals will arrange to have the Divisional H.Q. flag staff erected, and ensure that it is visible from Infantry Advanced Brigade H. Qrs.

L.A. Newnham Capt.
for
Lieut-Colonel,
General Staff.

Head Qrs. 56th Divn.
6th April, 1917.

Copies to -

167th Infantry Brigade
168th Infantry Brigade.
169th Infantry Brigade.
14th Division.
30th Division.
C.R.A.
C.R.E.
1/5th Cheshire Regt.
A.P.M.
193rd Div. M.G.Coy.
56th Div. Signals.

No. 8 Squadron R.F.C.
Div. M.G.Officer.
Div. Gas Officer.
G.O.C.
A.D.C.
A.D.M.S.
"Q"
War Diary.
File.

App VI

LOCATION TABLE.

APRIL	1	2	3	4	5	6	7	8	9	10	11	12	13	14	15
Div. H.Q.	BEAUMETZ-les-LOGES							AGNY	M3d51						
167th Inf. Bde. H.Q.	MONCHIET							RIGHT		LINE					
1st Ldn. Rgt.	MONCHIET	Reserve	AGNY		R	R	R	Support	R	R	Support				
3rd " "	MONCHIET	Support in Old British Line			AGNY	L	L	R	L	L	L				
7th M.x. "					Support. O.B. Line			Reserve		Support	R.centre		Reserve		
8th " "	MONCHIET	R	R	R	AGNY			L			L centre				
168th Inf. Bde. H.Q.	GOUY en Artois	M3b35.95					G33c	LEFT				Support			
4th Ldn. Rgt.	O.B.L.	ACHICOURT (reserve)		L	L	L	L	Reserve		Support	Reserve				
12th " "	GOUY	L	L	ACHICOURT				L	L	L					
13th " "	GOUY	Support		ACHICOURT				R	R	R					
14th " "	AGNY	ACHICOURT (reserve)	O.B. line					Support							
169th Inf. Bde. H.Q.	M3b39	MONCHIET						ACHICOURT MILL							
2nd Ldn. Rgt.	R	BEAUMETZ					OBL	BEAURAINS Reserve							
5th Ldn. Rgt.	ACHICOURT Support	MONCHIET					OBL	Area		Support	R. Support	R	Support	Support	
9th " "	R	MONCHIET					ACHICOURT			R	L	L	L	L	
13th " "	L	MONCHIET						Support			R	R	Support	R	
											L. Support	L. Support			
Div. Arty. H.Q.	BEAUMETZ-les-LOGES							AGNY	M3d51						
280 Bde.	Line														
281 "	Line														
Pioneers	ARRAS (Boulevard Crespel)							LINE							

← Relief on night 1/2 Apr.

LOCATION TABLE.

April	16	17	18	19	20	21	22	23	24	25	26	27	28	29	30
Div. H.Q.	AGNY	M3dSI		COUIN						HAUTEVILLE WARLUS				ARRAS At R.de la Pous	
167th Inf. Bde. H.Q.								GRENAS						LINE	LEFT
1st Ldn. Rgt.	SUPPORT	SUPPORT	ARRAS	POMMIER				HALLOY		HABARCQ DUISANS			SUPPORT	SUPPORT	
3rd. "				LACAPELLE				POMMERA							
7th M.X. "				BERLES				HALLOY					RESERVE	RESERVE	
8th "				LACAPELLE BERLES				MONDICOURT							LINE
168th. Inf. Bde H.Q.	LINE					COUIN									
4th. Ldn. Rgt.	R RESERVE	SUPPORT R L	ARRAS			BAYENCOURT			GOUY		SIMENCOURT			RESERVE ARRAS	
12th " "						COUIN									
13th " "	SUPPORT					BAYENCOURT									
14th " "	L	RESERVE				COIGNEUX									
169th. Inf. Bde. H.Q.	RESERVE	RESERVE			SOUASTRE				SOUASTRE WANQUETIN						RIGHT
2nd Ldn. Rgt.					ST AMAND						BERNEVILLE				
5th Ldn. Rgt.					BIENVILLERS								SUPPORT	SUPPORT	L
9th " "					SOUASTRE										R
13th " "					ST AMAND										
Div. Arty. H.Q.	AGNY	M3dSI			BEAUMETZ les LOGES										
280 Fde.	LINE	LINE			atd. VII Corps										
281 LINE	LINE	LINE			atd. VII Corps										
Pioneers	NEUVILLE VITASSE AREA	WAILLY		SOUASTRE					WANQUETIN					ARRAS	

VII Corps G.C.R.604/398.   56th Divn. G.3/121.

G.O.C.
   56th Division.

       The Corps Commander takes the opportunity, when the 56th Division is going back for a short rest, to congratulate you and your Division on the excellent work performed during the successful operation since Easter Sunday. It is needless for him to refer to the splendid way the Division fought, as their fighting qualities were fully proved at GOMMECOURT, and later on the SOMME. It is sufficient to note that the Division not only maintained but added to its reputation and this in very unpleasant circumstances in regard to weather. The Corps Commander hopes to have the honour of soon again including the Division in his Command.

19th April, 1917.   (Sgd.) J.BURNETT STUART,
                                                 Brigadier-General,
                                        General Staff, VIIth Corps.
                              2.

167th Infantry Brigade.   56th Div. M.G.Officer.
168th Infantry Brigade.   56th Div. Gas Officer.
169th Infantry Brigade.   A.D.M.S.
1/5th Cheshire Regiment.   D.A.D.O.S.
C.R.A.   A.D.V.S.
C.R.E.   4th Aust.Div.Supply Column.
A.P.M.   No. 2 Ammn. Sub Park.
193rd Div.M.G.Coy.   "Q"
56th Div.Signals.   War Diary.
56th Div. Train.   File.

       The General Officer Commanding has great pleasure in forwarding the above, and wishes to add that he is very proud of the fighting qualities of the Division and of its high standard of efficiency.

                                                           B. Pakenham

Head Qrs. 56th Divn.   Lieut-Colonel,
20th April, 1917.   General Staff.

G.

CASUALTIES.

PERIOD.	KILLED.		WOUNDED.		MISSING.		TOTALS.	
	O.	O.R.	O.	O.R.	O.	O.R.	O.	O.R.
April 5th – 8th.	2	35	9	156	—	26	11	217
" 9th.	7	192	30	623	—	29	37	844
" 10th – 13th.	4	65	19	223	—	10	23	298
" 14th.	5	43	16	391	3	271	24	705
" 15th – 22nd.	3	35	10	169	—	6	13	210
TOTALS.	21	370	84	1562	3	342	108	2274

write overleaf.

CASUALTIES.

UNIT	April 5th-8th					April 9th.					April 10th-13th.					April 14th					April 15th-22nd.					Total				
	K.		W.		M.	K.		W.		M.	K.		W.		M.	K.		W.		M.	K.		W.		M.	K.		W.		M.
	O.	O.R.	O.	O.R.	O.R.	O.	O.R.	O.	O.R.	O.R.	O.	O.R.	O.	O.R.	O.R.	O.	O.R.	O.	O.R.	O.R.	O.	O.R.	O.	O.R.	O.R.	O.	O.R.	O.	O.R.	O.R.
1st London Rgt.	-	4	-	6	-	1	18	4	87	14	-	-	-	1	-	-	-	-	-	-	-	-	-	-	-	1	22	10	150	31
3rd "	-	-	-	6	17	-	10	3	54	1	-	16	2	70	1	-	-	-	-	-	-	-	-	-	-	2	26	5	124	6
7th Middlesex.	-	-	-	4	-	-	12	3	57	1	1	14	5	27	-	-	-	-	-	-	-	-	-	1	-	2	26	8	89	-
8th "	-	-	-	-	-	2	19	4	121	3	-	11	5	15	-	-	-	-	1	-	-	-	-	-	-	2	30	7	136	6
4th London Rgt.	-	4	-	22	-	-	3	3	18	-	-	1	1	18	-	-	-	-	-	-	-	-	-	-	2	-	1	20	6	100	2
12th "	-	2	-	7	-	2	30	6	124	4	-	-	-	8	-	-	1	-	19	42	-	-	-	-	-	2	85	7	155	4
13th "	-	1	-	5	2	1	30	4	86	2	-	-	-	-	-	-	1	5	34	-	-	-	-	1	-	1	35	5	132	7
14th "	-	5	-	8	-	-	17	5	63	4	-	-	-	-	-	-	1	4	9	43	-	-	-	-	-	1	31	5	114	5
2nd "	-	-	-	-	-	-	-	-	-	-	-	9	1	18	-	-	-	-	9	-	-	-	-	-	-	-	14	2	25	-
5th "	-	2	-	-	-	-	-	1	8	-	1	5	2	20	7	-	5	-	40	7	-	-	-	-	-	2	12	1	60	8
9th "	-	2	-	3	-	-	-	-	-	-	-	8	5	25	-	-	1	24	10	206	149	-	-	-	-	-	1	34	18	234	149
15th "	-	12	1	27	7	-	-	-	8	-	-	2	1	11	-	3	6	8	135	3	115	-	-	-	-	4	20	6	173	5/122
5th Cheshires.	-	1	-	6	-	-	-	-	-	1	1	-	-	2	-	-	-	-	-	-	1	-	-	-	-	1	-	1	8	-
167th M.G.Coy.	-	-	-	-	-	-	-	-	-	-	-	-	-	-	-	-	-	-	-	1	-	-	-	-	-	-	-	-	-	-
168th "	-	1	-	1	-	-	-	-	-	-	-	1	-	5	-	-	-	-	-	-	-	-	-	-	-	-	2	-	4	-
169th "	-	1	1	2	-	-	-	-	-	-	-	-	1	7	-	-	-	-	-	-	-	-	-	-	-	-	-	1	3	-
195rd "	-	-	-	-	-	-	1	2	-	2	-	2	-	-	-	-	-	-	-	-	-	-	-	-	-	-	3	-	3	-
168th T.M.Bty.	-	-	-	1	-	-	-	-	-	-	-	-	-	5	-	-	-	-	-	1	-	-	-	-	-	-	-	2	-	6	-
280th Bde. RFA.	-	-	1	-	-	-	-	-	-	-	-	-	-	-	-	-	-	-	-	-	-	-	-	-	-	3	-	4	3	-
281st "	-	-	-	3	-	-	-	-	-	-	-	-	-	-	-	-	-	-	-	-	-	-	-	-	-	3	-	-	3	-
D.A.C. (RE																														
416 (Edin)Fld Cy	-	-	1	18	-	-	2	-	-	-	-	-	-	-	-	-	-	-	1	-	-	-	-	-	-	1	2	6	-	7
512 (Lond) "	-	1	-	4	-	-	-	-	-	-	-	-	-	-	-	-	-	-	-	-	-	-	-	-	-	-	-	-	3	-
Divl.Sig.Coy.	-	-	-	2	-	-	-	-	-	-	-	-	-	-	-	-	-	-	-	-	-	-	-	1	-	-	-	3	-	-
Divl.Train.	-	-	-	-	-	-	-	-	-	-	-	-	-	-	-	-	-	-	-	-	-	-	-	-	-	-	-	-	-	-
2/3rd Ldn.Fld.Amb.	-	1	-	-	-	-	-	-	-	-	-	-	-	-	-	-	-	-	-	-	-	-	-	-	-	-	-	-	1	-
TOTALS.	2	35	9	156	26	7	192	30	625	29	4	65	19	225	10	5	43	18	591	3	271	3	35	10	199	6	24 519 84 1763 2342

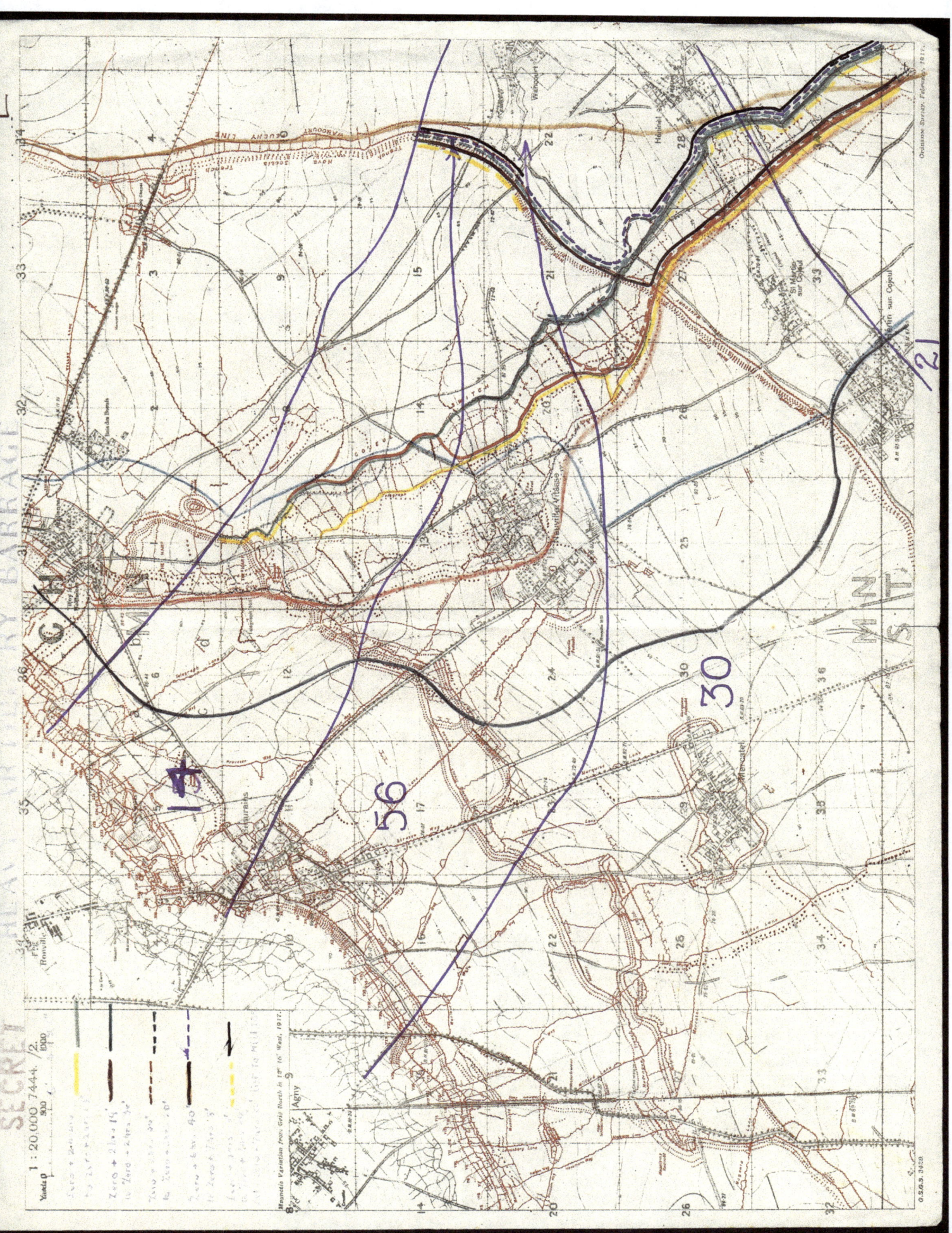

Identification Trace for use with Artillery Maps.

N O

BRIGADE BOUNDARY
DIVISIONAL BOUNDARY
GORDON ALLEY
GORDON ALLEY COMMON TO BOTH BDES.

NOTE.—(1). These traces are intended to facilitate the communication of information as to the position of targets, which have been located on a squared map.
(2). The squares on this trace are 500 yards in length on the 1/10,000 scale, 1,000 yards in length on the 1/20,000 scale, and 2,000 yards in length on the 1/40,000 scale.
(3). The squares on the trace are fitted to the squares of the map showing the targets, which are then drawn on the trace. Sufficient letters and numbers must also be added to enable the recipient to place the trace in the correct position on his own map. A little detail may also be traced, but this is not essential. The name and scale of the map to which the trace refers must be always given. The trace can be used for the 1/10,000, 1/20,000, or 1/40,000 scale.

G.S.G.S. 3025.

Tracing taken from Sheet 51.b S.W. Ed.4
of the 1: 20,000 map of
Signature   Date

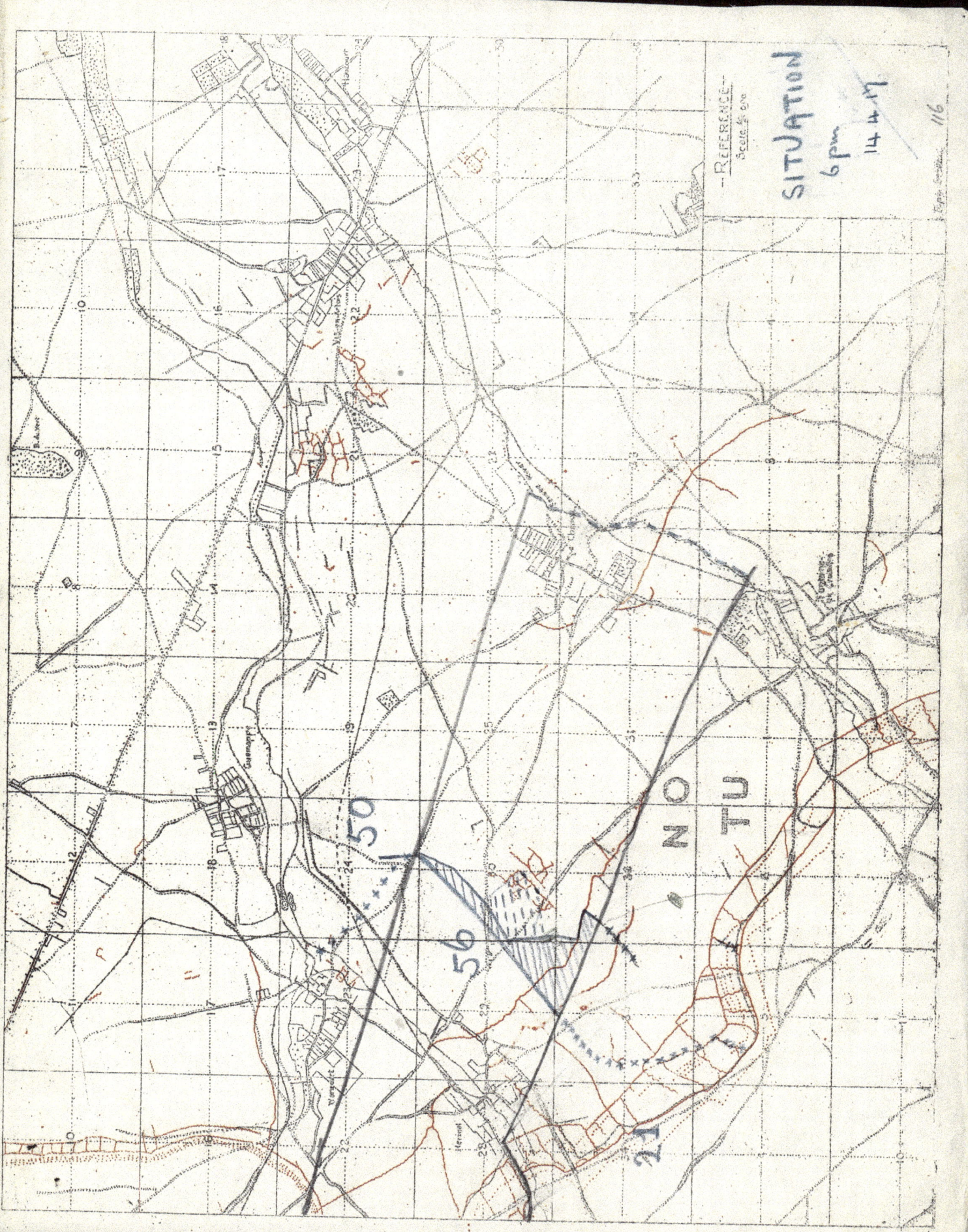

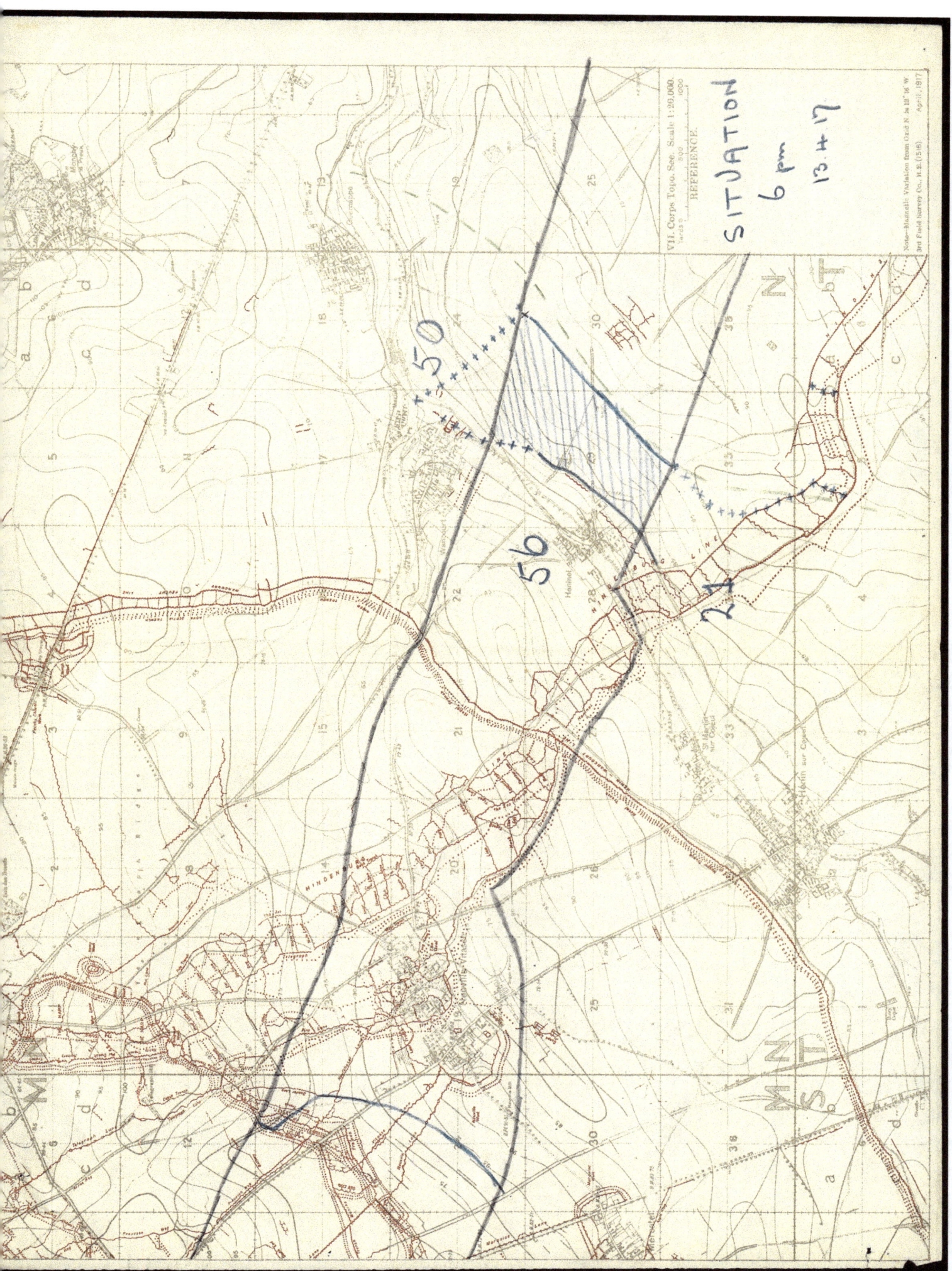

Nouv. Vitt. (2)

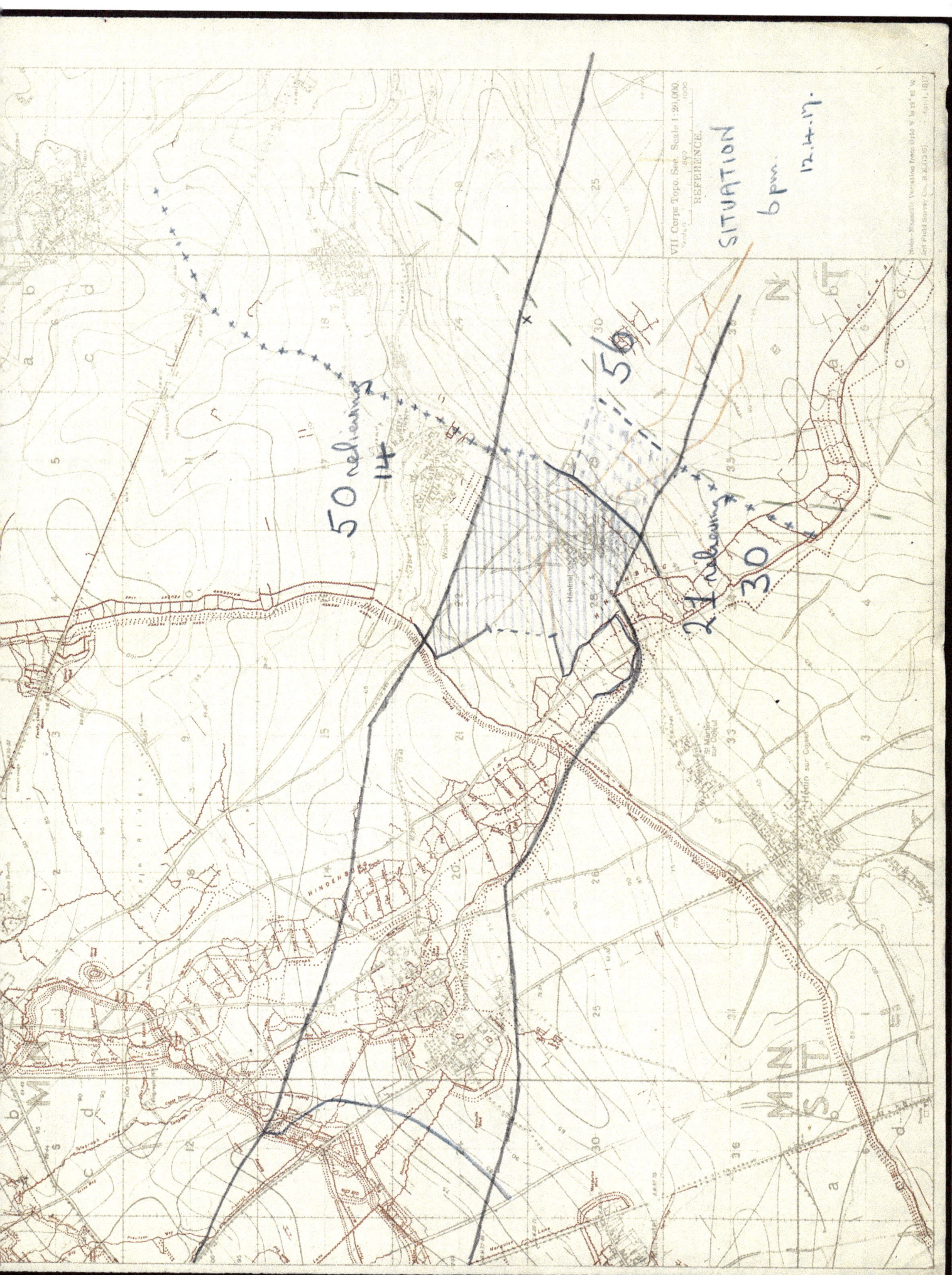

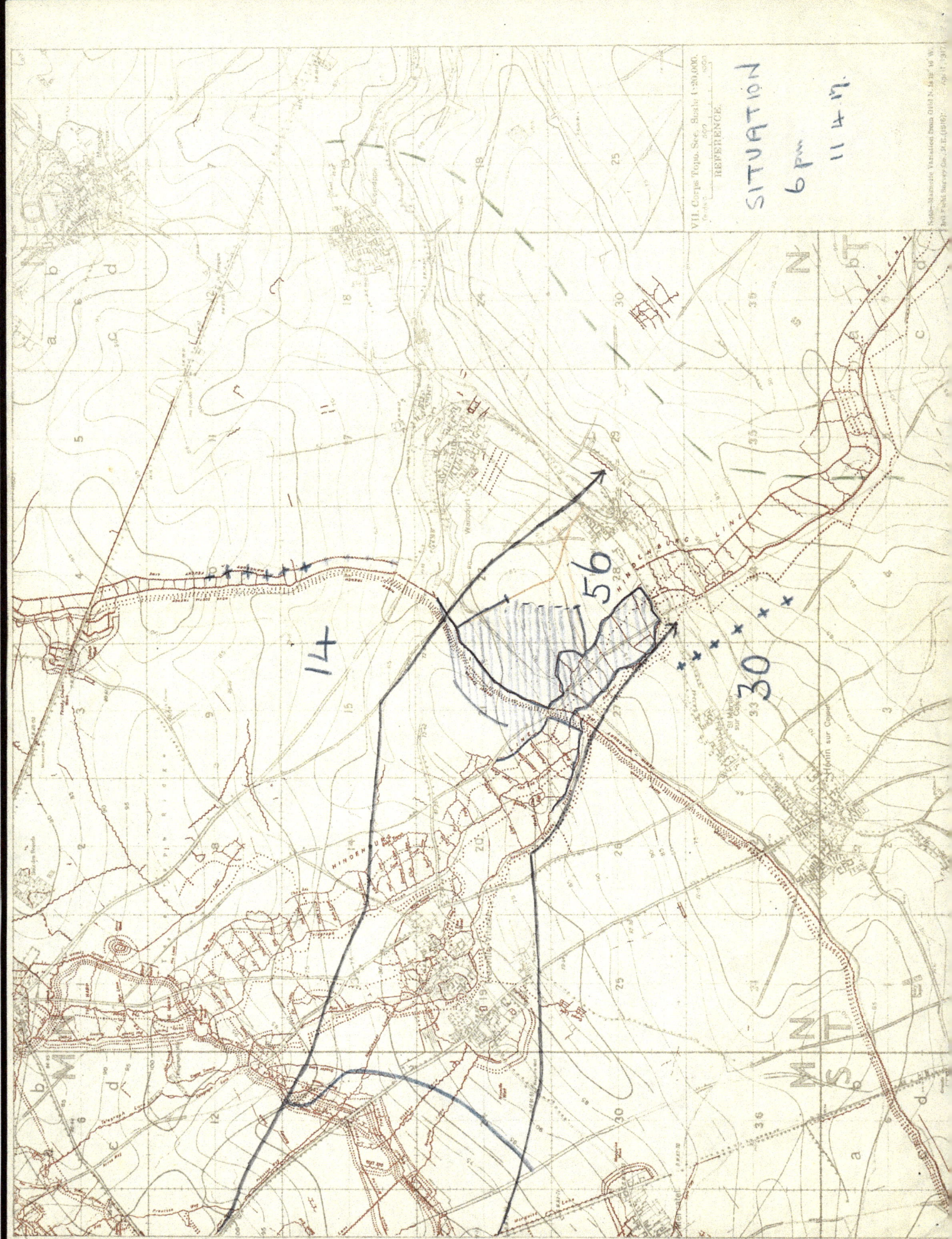

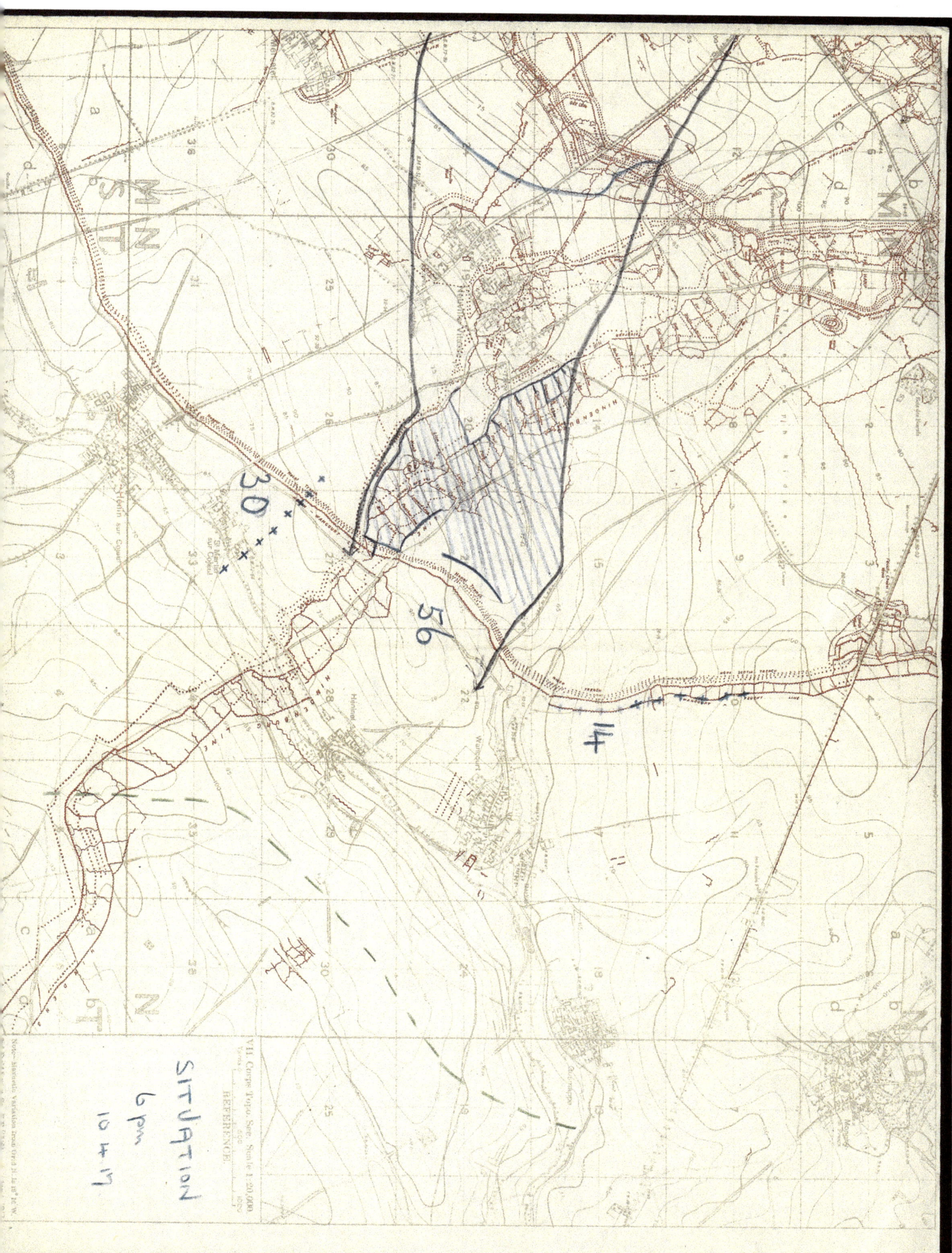

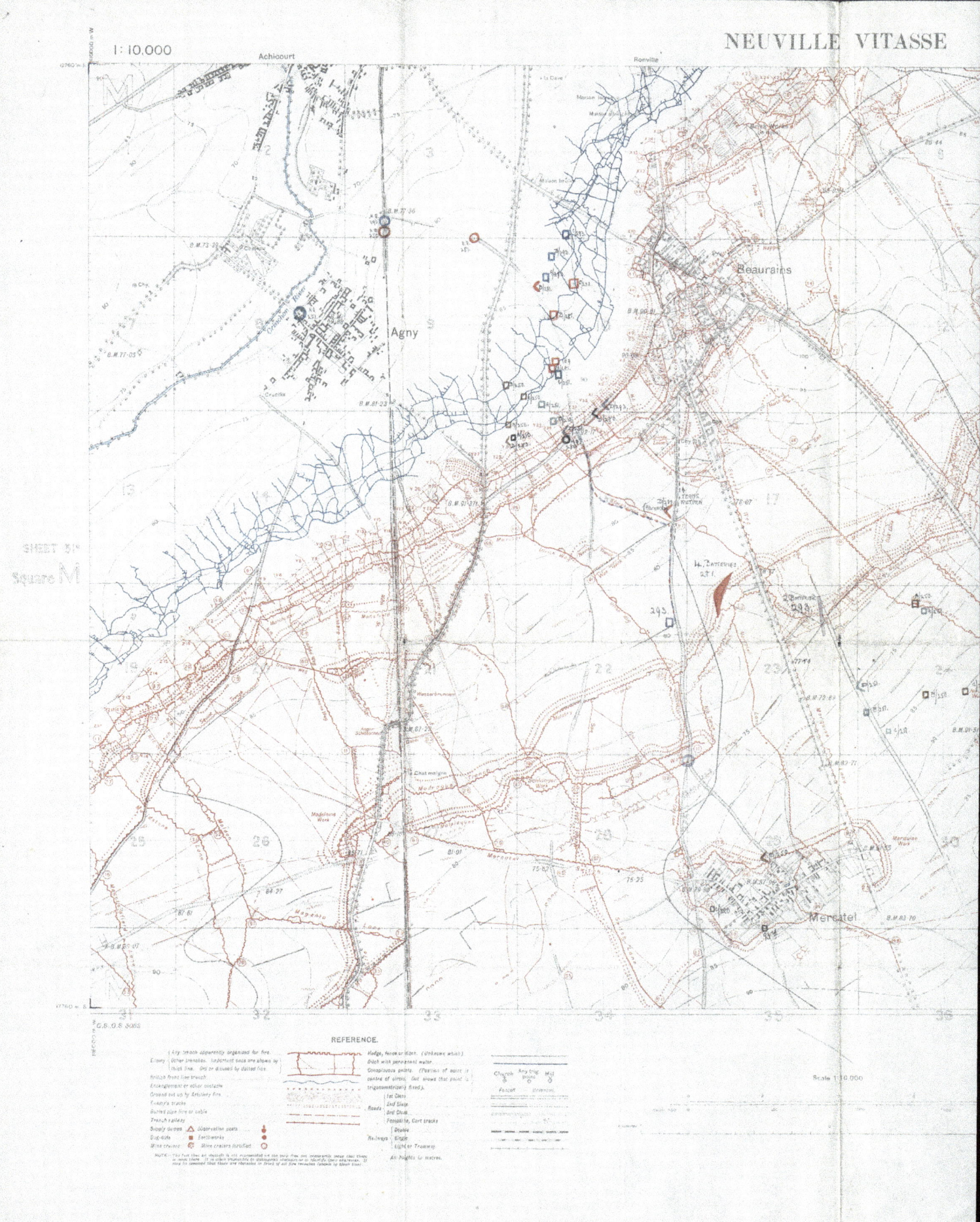

GLOSSARY.

Abbaye, Abb^e	Abbey.
Abreuvoir, Ab^r	Watering-place.
Abri de douaniers	Customs-shelter.
Aciérie	Steel works.
Aiguille	Points (Ry.)
Allée	Alley, Narrow road.
Ancien-ne, Anc^{n-ne}	Old.
Aqueduc	Aqueduct.
Arbre	Tree.
" éventail	" fan-shaped.
" décharné	" bare.
" fourchu	" forked.
" isolé	" isolated.
" penché	" leaning.
Arbrisseau	Small tree.
Arc	Arch.
Ardoisière, Ard^{re}	Slate quarry.
Arrêt	Halt.
Asile	Asylum.
" des aliénés	Lunatic asylum.
" d'aliénée	
" de charité	
" des pauvres	Asylum.
" de refuge	
Auberge, Aub^e	Inn.
Aune	Alder-tree.
Bac	Ferry.
" à traille	
Bains	Baths.
Place aux bains	Bathing place.
Balise	Bcon, Beacon.
Banc de sable	Sand-bank.
" " vase	Mud-bank.
Baraque	Hut.
Barrage	Dam.
Barrière	Gate, Stile.
Machine à) Bascule	Weigh-bridge.
Bassin	Dock, Pond.
" d'échouage	Tidal dock.
Bassin de radoub	Dry dock.
Bateau phare	Light ship.
Blanchisserie	Laundry.
B.M. (borne militaire)	Mile stone.
B^e (borne kilométrique)	
Boutonnerie	Belt Factory.
Fab^e de boutons	
Bouée	Buoy.
Brasserie, Brass^e	Brewery.
Briqueterie, Briq^{ie}	Brickfield.
Brise-lames	Breakwater.
Bureau de poste	Post office.
Bureau de douane	Custom house.
Butte	Butt, Mound.
Cabane	Hut.
Cabaret, Cab^t	Inn.
Câble sous-marin	Submarine cable.
Calvaire, Calv^{re}	Calvary.
Canal de desséchement	Drainage canal.
Canal d'irrigation	Irrigation canal.
Fab^e de caoutchouc	Rubber factory.
Carrière, Carr^{re}	Quarry.
" de gravier	Gravel-pit.
Caserne	Barracks.
Champ de courses	Race course.
" " manœuvres	Drill-ground.
" " tir	Rifle range.
	Building yard.
Chantier	Ship yard.
	Dock yard.
Chantier de construction	Slip-way.
Chapelle, Ch^{le}	Chapel.
Charbonnage	Colliery.
Château d'eau	Water tower.
Chaussée	Causeway.
	Highway.
Chemin de fer	Railway.
Cheminée, Ch^{ée}	Chimney.
Chêne	Oak tree.
Cimetière, Cim^{re}	Cemetery.
Clocher	Belfry.
Clouterie	Nail factory.
Colombier	Dove-cot.
Coton	
Cour des marchandises	Goods yard.
Couvent	Convent.
Crassier	Slag heap.
Croix	Cross.
Darse	Inner dock.
Démoli-e, Dém^e	Destroyed.
Déversoir	Weir.
Digue	Dyke, causeway.
Distillerie, Dist^{ie}	Distillery.
Douane	
Bureau de douane	Custom-house.
Entrepôt de douane	Custom warehouse.
Dynamitière, Dynam^{re}	Dynamite magasin.
Dynamiterie	Dynamite factory.
Ecluse	Sluice, Lock.
Ecluzette, Ecl^{tte}	Sluice.
Ecole	School.
Ecurie	Stable.
Eglise	Church.
Emaillerie	Enamel works.
Embarcadère, Emb^{re}	Landing-place.
Estaminet, Estam^t	Inn.
Etang	Pond.
Fabrique, Fab^e	Factory.
Fab^e de produits chimiques	Chemical works.
Fab^e de faïence	Pottery.
Faïencerie	
Ferme, F^{me}	Farm.
Filature, Fil^{re}	Spinning mill.
Fonderie, Fond^{ie}	Foundry.
Fontaine, Font^{ne}	Spring, fountain.
Forêt	Forest.
Forme de radoub	Dry dock.
Forge	Smithy.
Fosse	Mine, Pit.
Fossé	Moat, Ditch.
Four	Kiln.
" à chaux	Lime-kiln.
Four à coke	Coke oven.
Ganterie	Glove Factory.
Gare	Station.
Garenne	Warren.
Garnison	Garrison.
Gazomètre	Gasometer.
Glacerie	
Fab^e de glaces	Mirror Factory.
Glacière	Ice factory.
Grue	Crane.
Gué	Ford.
Guérite	Sentry-box, Turret.
" à signaux	Signal-box (Ry.)
Halte	Halt.
Hangar	Shed, Hangar.
Hôpital	Hospital.
Hôtel-de-Ville	Town hall.
Houillère	Colliery.
Huilerie	Oil factory.
Imprimerie, Impr^{ie}	Printing works.
Jetée	Pier.
Laminerie	Rolling mills.
Ligne de haute marée	High water mark.
Laisse de basse marée	Low
Maison Forestière	Forester's house.
M^{on} F^{re}	
Malterie	Malt-house.
Marbrerie	Marble works.
Marais	Marsh.
Marais salant	Saltern.
	Salt marsh.
Marché	Market.
Mare	Pool.
Meule	Rick.
Minière	Mine.
Monastère	Monastery.
Moulin, Mⁱⁿ	Mill.
" à vapeur	Steam mill.
Mur	Wall.
" crénelé	Loop-holed wall.
Nacelle	
Orme	
Orphelinat	Orphanage.
Oseraies	
Ouvrage	
Ouvrages hydrauliques	
Papeterie	
Parc	
" aérostatique	
" à charbon	
" à pétrole	
Passage à niveau P.N.	
Passerelle, Pass^{re}	
Pépinière	
Peuplier	
Phare	
Pilier, Pil^r	
Plaine d'exercice	
Pompe	
Ponceau	
Pont	
" levis	
Poste de garde	
Station côte	
Potean P^u	
Poterie	
Poudrière, Poud^{re}	
Magasin à poudre	
Prise d'eau	
Puits	
" artésien	
" d'aérage	
" ventilateur	
" de sondage	
Quai	
" aux bestiaux	
" aux marchandises	
Raccordement	
Raffinerie	
" de sucre	
Râperie	

coke	Coke oven.
	Glove Factory.
	Station.
	Warren.
	Garrison.
	Gasometer.
glaces	Mirror Factory.
	Ice factory.
	Crane.
	Ford.
	Sentry-box, Turret.
à signaux	Signal-box (Ry.)
	Halt.
	Shed, Hangar.
	Hospital.
-Ville	Town hall.
	Colliery.
	Oil factory.
rie Imp{rie}	Printing works.
	Pier.
	Rolling mills.
de haute marée	High water mark.
de basse marée	Low " "
Forestière	Forester's house.
	Malt-house.
rie	Marble works.
	Marsh.
salant	Saltern.
	Salt marsh.
	Market.
	Post.
	Rick.
	Mine.
ère	Monastery.
M{in}	Mill.
à vapeur	Steam mill.
	Wall.
nelé	Loop-holed wall.

Nacelle	Ferry.
Orme	Elm.
Orphelinat	Orphanage.
Osseraie	Osier-beds.
Ouvrages	Fort.
Ouvrages hydrauliques	Water works.
Papeterie	Paper-mill.
Parc	Park, yard.
" aérostatique	Aviation ground.
" à charbon	Coal yard.
" à pétrole	Petrol store.
Passage à niveau P.N.	Level-crossing.
Passerelle, Pas{lle}	Foot-bridge.
Pépinière	Nursery-garden.
Peuplier	Poplar tree.
Phare	Light-house.
Pilier, Pil{r}	Post.
Plaine d'exercice	Drill ground.
Pompe	Pump.
Ponceau	Culvert.
Pont	Bridge.
" levis	Drawbridge.
Poste de garde	Coast-guard
Station côte	station.
Poteau P{re}	Post.
Poterie	Pottery.
Poudrière, Poud{re}	Powder magazine.
Magasin à poudre	
Prise d'eau	Water supply.
Puits	Pit-head, Shaft, Well.
" artésien	Artesian well.
" d'aérage	
" ventilateur	Ventilating shaft.
" de sondage	Boring.
Quai	Quay, Platform.
" aux bestiaux	Cattle platform.
" aux marchandises	Goods platform.
Raccordement	Junction.
Raffinerie	Refinery.
" de sucre	Sugar refinery
Rîperie	Beet-root factory.

Remblai	Embankment.
Remise {dos aux} Machines	Engine-shed.
Réservoir, Rés{r}	Reservoir.
Route cavalière	Bridle road.
Rubanerie	Ribbon Factory.
Ruine	
Ruines	Ruin.
En ruine	
Ruiné -e	
Sablière	Sand-pit.
Sablonnière, Sablon{re}	
Sapin	Fir tree.
Saule	Willow tree.
Saunerie	Salt-works.
Scierie, Sc{ie}	Saw-mill.
Sondage	Boring.
Source	Spring.
Sucrerie, Suc{ie}	Sugar factory.
Tannerie	Tannery.
Tir à la cible	Rifle range.
Tissage	Weaving mill.
Tôlerie	Rolling mill.
Tombeau	Tomb.
Tour	Tower.
Tourbière	Peat-bog, Peat-bed.
Tourelle	Small tower.
Tuilerie	Tile works.
Usine à gaz	Gas works.
" électrique	
" d'électricité	Electricity works.
" métallurgique	Metal works.
" à agglomérés	Briquette factory.
Verrerie, Verr{ie}	Glass works.
Viaduc	Viaduct.
Vivier	Fish Pond.
Voie de chargement	
" déchargement	
" d'évitement	Siding.
" formation	
" manœuvre	
Zinguerie	Zinc works.

TRENCH MAP
NEUVILLE VITASSE
51B S.W. 1.
EDITION 5. A
Scale 1:10,000.

INDEX TO ADJOINING SHEETS.

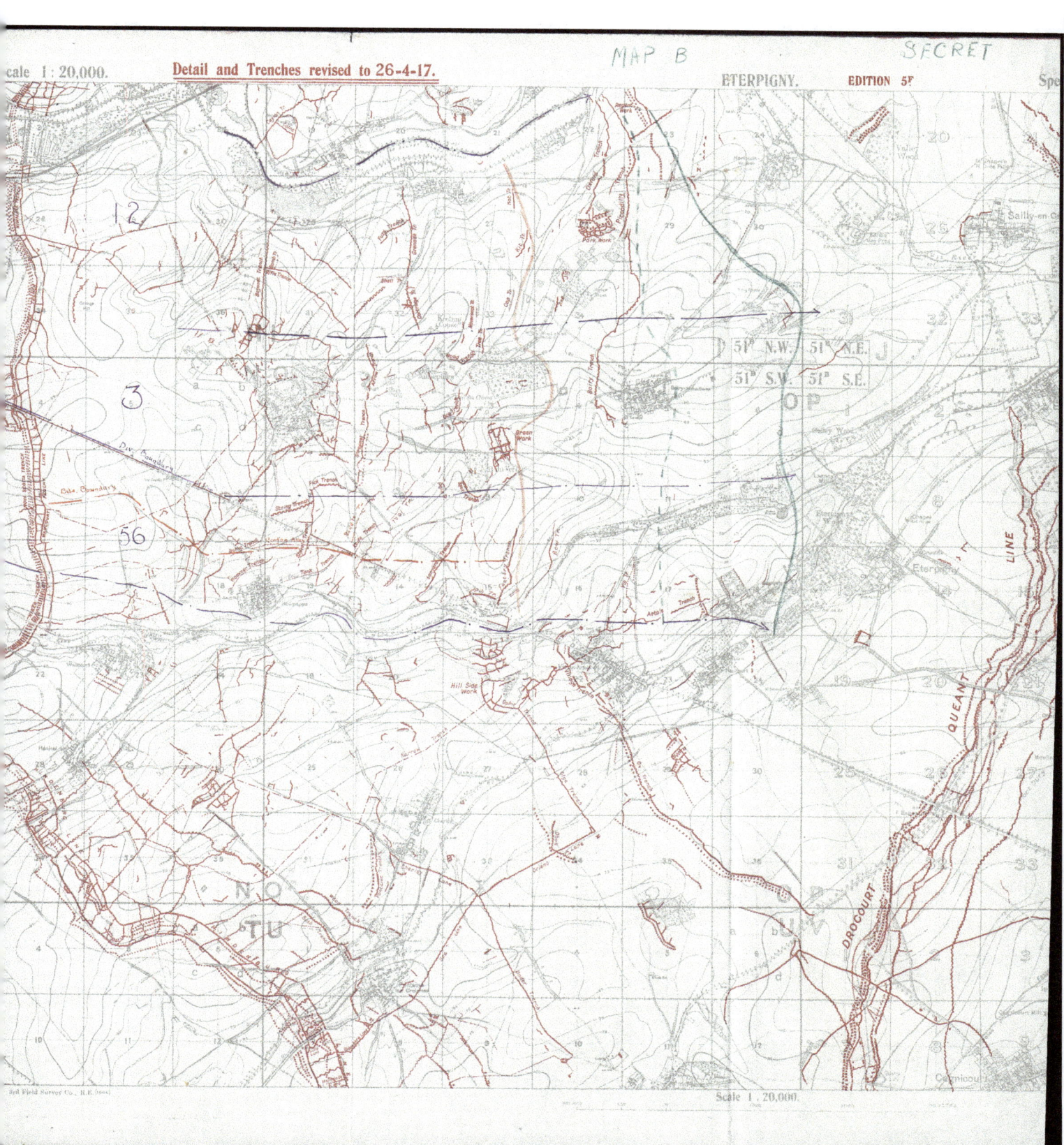

GLOSSARY.

Abbaye, Abb^e	Abbey.
Abreuvoir, Ab^r	Watering-place.
Abri de douaniers	Customs shelter.
Aciérie	Steel works.
Aiguille	Point (Is.)
Allée	Alley, Narrow road
Ancien, -ne, Anc^n	Old.
Aqueduc	Aqueduct.
Arbre	Tree.
„ éventail	„ fan-shaped.
„ fourchu	„ forked.
„ isolé	„ isolated.
„ penché	„ leaning.
Arbrisseau	Small tree.
Arc	Arch.
Ardoisière, Ard^re	Slate quarry.
Arrêt	Halt.
Asile	Asylum.
„ des aliénés	Lunatic asylum.
„ d' „	
„ de charité	
„ des pauvres	Asylum.
„ de refuge	
Auberge, Aub^e	Inn.
Aune	Alder-tree.
Bac	Ferry.
„ à traille	
Bains	Baths.
Bains sur bains	Bathing place.
Balise	Boom, Beacon.
Banc de sable	Sand-bank.
„ vase	Mud-bank.
Baraque	Hut.
Barrage	Dam.
Bascule	Gate, Stile.
(Machine à) Bascule	Weigh-bridge.
Bassin	Dock, Pond.
„ d'échouage	Tidal dock.
Bassin de radoub	Dry dock.
Bateau phare	Light-ship.
Blanchisserie	Laundry.
B.M. (borne militaire)	Mile stone.
B^e (borne kilométrique)	
Boulonnerie	Bolt-Factory.
Fab^e de boulons	
Bouée	Buoy.
Brasserie, Brass^e	Brewery.
Briqueterie, Briq^e	Brickfield.
Brise-lames	Breakwater.
Bureau de poste	Post office.
„ de douane	Custom house.
Butte	Butt, Mound.
Cabane	Hut.
Cabaret, Cab^t	Inn.
Câble sous-marin	Submarine cable.
Calvaire, Cal^re	Calvary.
Canal de dessèchement	Drainage canal.
Canal d'irrigation	Irrigation canal.
Fab^e de caoutchouc	Rubber factory.
Carrière, Carr^e	Quarry.
„ de gravier	Gravel-pit.
Caserne	Barracks.
Champ de courses	Race-course.
„ manœuvres	Drill ground.
„ tir	Rifle range.
Chantier	Building yard.
„	Ship yard.
„	Dock yard.
Chantier de construction	Slip-way.
Chapelle, Ch^le	Chapel.
Charbonnage	Colliery.
Château d'eau	Water tower.
Chaussée	Causeway, Highway.
Chemin de fer	Railway.
Cheminée, Ch^ée	Chimney.
Chêne	Oak tree.
Cimetière, Cim^re	Cemetery.
Clocher	Belfry.
Clouterie	Nail factory.
Colombier	Dove-cot.
Coron	Workmen's dwellings.
Cour des marchandises	Goods yard.
„ aux	
Couvent	Convent.
Créneau	Flag, heap.
Croix	Cross.
Darse	Inner dock.
Démoli -e	Destroyed.
Détroit -e, Dét^t	
Déversoir	Weir.
Digue	Dyke, causeway.
Distillerie, Dist^e	Distillery.
Douane	Custom-house.
Bureau de douane	
Entrepôt de douane	Custom warehouse.
Dynamitière, Dynam^re	Dynamite magazine.
Dynamiterie	Dynamite factory.
Écluse	Sluice, Lock.
Échauette, Éch^te	Shrine.
École	School.
Écurie	Stable.
Église	Church.
Émaillerie	Enamel works.
Embarcadère, Emb^re	Landing-place.
Estaminet, Estam^t	Inn.
Étang	Pond.
Fabrique, Fab^e	Factory.
Fab^e de produits chimiques	Chemical works.
Fab^e de faïences	Pottery.
Faïencerie	
Ferme, F^me	Farm.
Filature, Fil^re	Spinning mill.
Fonderie, Fond^e	Foundry.
Fontaine, Font^ne	Spring, fountain.
Forêt	Forest.
Forme de radoub	Dry dock.
Forge	Smithy.
Fosse	Mine, Pit.
Fossé	Moat, Ditch.
Four	Kiln.
„ à chaux	Lime-kiln.
Four à coke	Coke oven.
Ganterie	Glove Factory.
Gare	Station.
Garenne	Warren.
Garnison	Garrison.
Gazomètre	Gasometer.
Glacerie	Mirror Factory.
Fab^e de glaces	
Glacière	Ice factory.
Grue	Crane.
Gué	Ford.
Guérite	Sentry-box, Turret
„ à signaux	Signal-box (Ry.)
Halte	Halt.
Hangar	Shed, Hangar.
Hôpital	Hospital.
Hôtel-de-Ville	Town hall.
Houillère	Colliery.
Huilerie	Oil factory.
Imprimerie, Impr^e	Printing works.
Jetée	Pier.
Laminerie	Rolling mills.
Ligne de haute marée	High water mark.
Laisse de basse marée	Low „
Maison Forestière, M^on F^re	Forester's house.
Malterie	Malt-house.
Marbrerie	Marble works.
Marais	Marsh.
Marais salant	Saltern, Salt marsh.
Marché	Market.
Mare	Pool.
Meule	Rick.
Minière	Mine.
Monastère	Monastery.
Moulin, M^in	Mill.
„ à vapeur	Steam mill.
Mur	Wall.
„ crénelé	Loop-holed wall.
Nacelle	Ferry.
Orme	Elm.
Orphelinat	Orphanage.
Oseraie	Osier-beds.
Ouvrage	Fort.
Ouvrages hydrauliques	Water works.
Papeterie	Paper-mill.
Parc	Park, yard.
„ aéronautique	Aviation ground.
„ à charbon	Coal yard.
„ à pétrole	Petrol store.
Passage à niveau P.N.	Level crossing.
Passerelle, Pass^le	Foot-bridge.
Pépinière	Nursery-garden.
Peuplier	Poplar tree.
Phare	Light-house.
Pilier, Pil^r	Post.
Plaine d'exercice	Drill ground.
Pompe	Pump.
Ponceau	Culvert.
Pont	Bridge.
„ levis	Drawbridge.
Poste de garde	Coast-guard station.
Station côte	
Poteau T^re	Post.
Poterie	Pottery.
Poudrière, Poud^re	Powder magazine.
Magasin à poudre	
Prise d'eau	Water supply.
Puits	Pit-head, Shaft, Well.
„ artésien	Artesian well.
„ d'aérage ventilateur	Ventilating shaft.
„ de sondage	Boring.
Quai	Quay, Platform.
„ aux bestiaux	Cattle platform.
„ aux marchandises	Goods platform.
Raccordement	Junction.
Raffinerie	Refinery.
„ de sucre	Sugar refinery.
Râperie	Beet-root factory.

TRENCH MAP.

FRANCE.
SHEET 51B S.W.
EDITION 4.A

INDEX TO ADJOINING SHEETS

SCALE 20,000

Four à coke	Coke oven
Ganterie	Glove Factory
Gare	Station
Garenne	Warren
Gazomètre	Gasometer
Glacerie	Mirror Factory
Fab. de glace	Ice factory
Glacière	Crane
Grue	Ford
Gué	Sentry-box, Turret
Guérite	Signal-box (Ry.)
à signaux	
Halte	Halt
Hangar	Shed, Hangar
Hôpital	Hospital
Hôtel-de-Ville	Town hall
Houillère	Colliery
Huilerie	Oil factory
Imprimerie, Imp.ᵉ	Printing works
Jetée	Pier
Lamineries	Rolling mills
Ligne de haute	High water mark
Laisse marée	
de basse marée	Low
Maison Forestière	Forester's house
Mᵒⁿ Fᵉʳᵉ	
Malterie	Malt-house
Marbrerie	Marble works
Marais	Marsh
Marais salant	Salt-pan, Salt marsh
Marché	Market
Mare	Pool
Meule	Rick
Minière	Mine
Monastère	Monastery
Moulin, Mᵏⁿ	Mill
à vapeur	Steam mill
Mur	Wall
crénelé	Loop-holed wall
Nacelle	Ferry
Orme	Elm
Orphelinat	Orphanage
Oseraies	Osier-beds
Ouvrages	Fort
Ouvrages hydrauliques	Water works
Papeterie	Paper-mill
Parc	Park, yard
aérostatique	Aviation ground
à charbon	Coal yard
à pétrole	Petrol store
Passage à niveau P.N.	Level-crossing
Passerelle, Padⁿ	Foot-bridge
Pépinière	Nursery-garden
Peuplier	Poplar tree
Phare	Light-house
Pilier, Pil.ʳ	Post
Plaine d'exercice	Drill ground
Pompe	Pump
Ponceau	Culvert
Pont	Bridge
levis	Drawbridge
Poste de garde	Coast-guard
Station côte	station
Poteau Pᵗᵉᵃ	Post
Poterie	Pottery
Poudrière, Poud.ᵉʳ	Powder magazine
Magasin à poudre	
Prise d'eau	Water supply
Puits	Pit-head, Shaft, Well
artésien	Artesian well
d'airage	
ventilateur	Ventilating shaft
de sondage	Boring
Quai	Quay, Platform
aux bestiaux	Cattle platform
aux marchandises	Goods platform
Raccordement	Junction
Raffinerie	Refinery
de sucre	Sugar refinery
Râperie	Beet-root factory
Remblai	Embankment
Remise des Machines	Engine-shed
Réservoir, Résᵛ	Reservoir
Route cavalière	Bridle road
Rubanerie	Ribbon Factory
Ruine	
Ruines	Ruin
En ruine	
Ruiné -e	
Sablière	Sand-pit
Sablonnière, Sablonⁿᵉ	
Sapin	Fir tree
Saule	Willow tree
Saunerie	Salt-works
Scierie, Scᵉ	Saw-mill
Sondage	Boring
Source	Spring
Sucrerie, Sucᵉ	Sugar factory
Tannerie	Tannery
Tir à la cible	Rifle range
Tissage	Weaving mill
Tôlerie	Rolling mill
Tombeau	Tomb
Tour	Tower
Tourbière	Peat-bog, Peat-bed
Tourelle	Small tower
Tuilerie	Tile works
Usine à gaz	Gas works
électrique d'électricité	Electricity works
métallurgique	Metal works
à agglomérés	Briquette factory
Verrerie, Verrᵉ	Glass works
Viaduc	Viaduct
Vivier	Fish Pond
Voie de chargement	
de déchargement	
d'évitement	Siding
de formation	
de manœuvre	
Zingerie	Zinc works

1. Brickfields.
2. Stone built, solid Chateau.
3. Very solid stone house.
4. Solid stone farm, with outhouses of brick, 18in. thick.
5. Big stone house.
6. Watering place.
7. Large solid brick and stone house.
8. Chateau and farm, former brick, latter stone, very strong.
9. Sugar factory, of brick, very solid.
10. Mairie, stone, very solid.
11. Watering place.
12. Big Chateau, with stables, outhouses, brick and stone, very strong.
13. Big stone built farm.
14. Large solid house, of stone.
15. Stone and brick Chateau.
16. Distillery, of brick, solid.
17. Chateau, brick, solid.
18. Big, solid, brick house.
19. Ditto.
20. Old windmill, with walls 2.35m. thick, very strong.
21. Church, with tower, strongly built.
22. Farm, large, of brick and stone, walls standing.
23. Farm, of brick, standing.
24. Brick building, solid.
25. Ditto.

WELLS.—Nearly every house has one (windlass) in its yard or just outside. Average depth 35m.

UNDERGROUND PASSAGES.—Deep and wide under house and grounds of pt. 12. Reported wide enough for cart and horse to drive along. Another reported connecting pts. 7 and 12.

NEUVILLE VITASSE

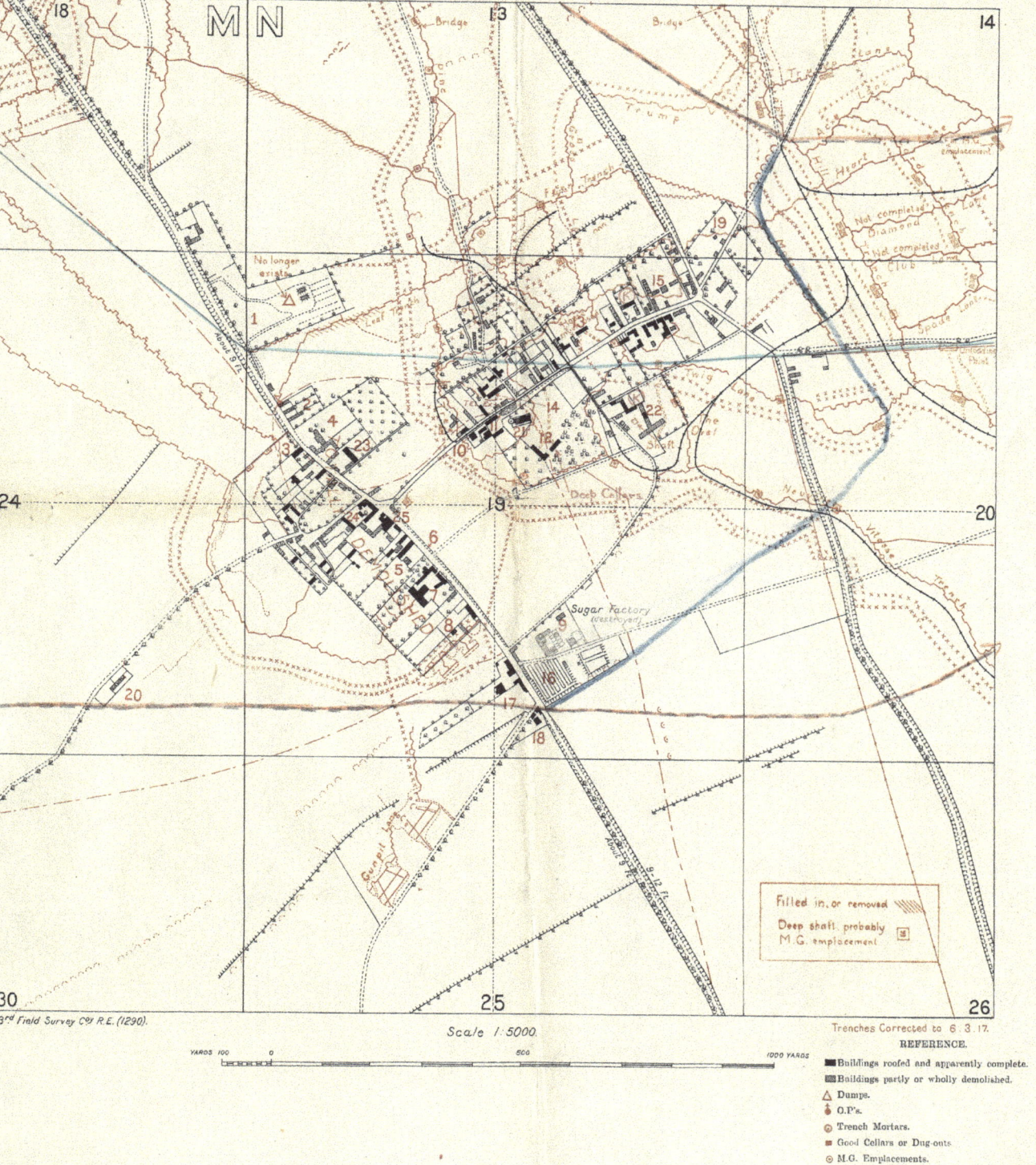

3rd Field Survey Coy R.E. (1290).

Scale 1:5000.

Trenches Corrected to 6.3.17.

REFERENCE.
- Buildings roofed and apparently complete.
- Buildings partly or wholly demolished.
- △ Dumps.
- O.P.'s.
- Trench Mortars.
- Good Cellars or Dug-outs.
- M.G. Emplacements.

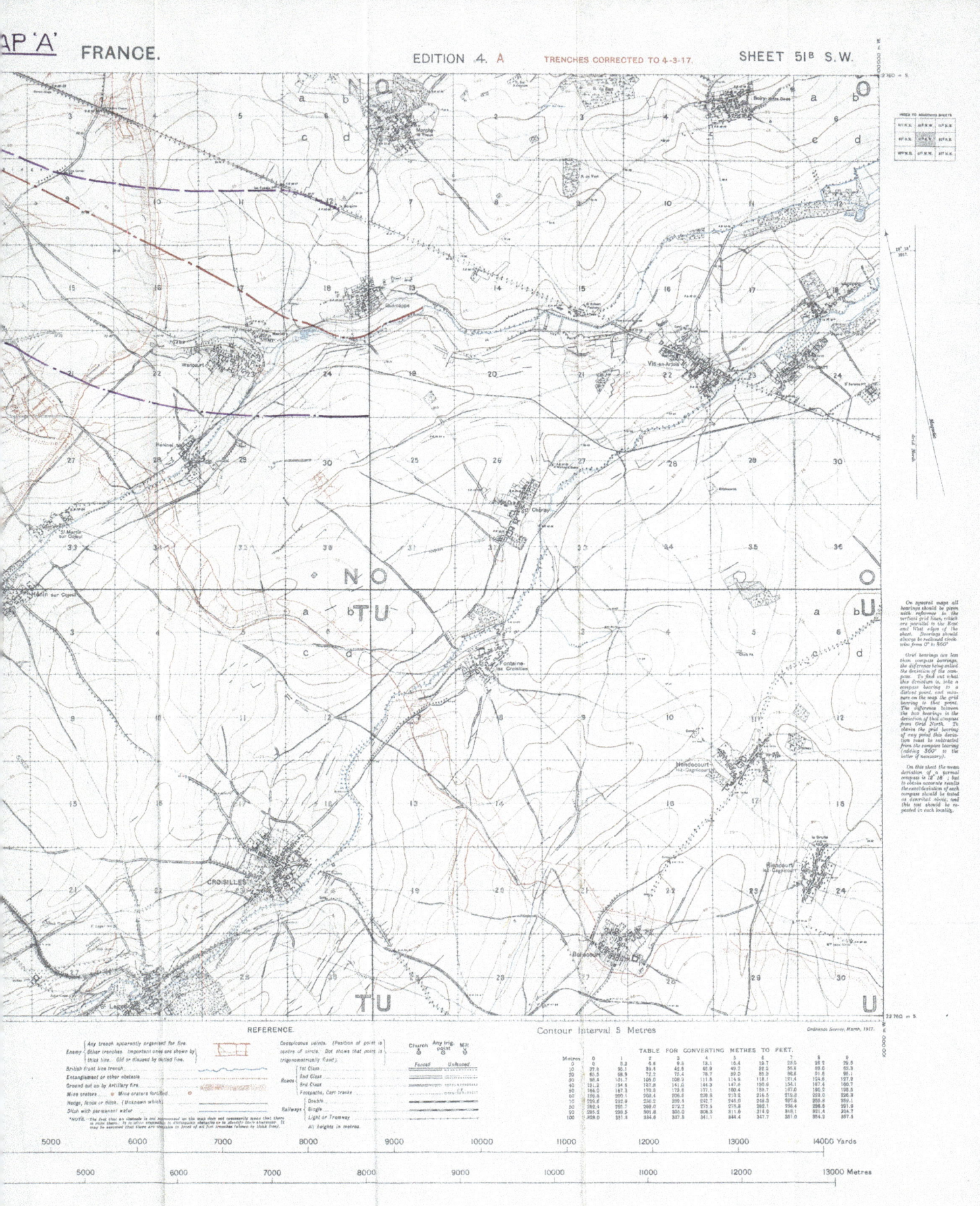

GLOSSARY.

Abbaye, Abb⁶	Abbey.
Abreuvoir, Ab⁶	Watering-place.
Abri de douaniers	Custom-shelter.
Aciérie	Steel works.
Aiguilles	Points (Ry.)
Allée	Alley, Narrow road
Ancien · ne, Anc⁶ · ⁿ⁶	Old.
Aqueduc	Aqueduct.
Arbre	Tree.
„ éventail	„ fan-shaped
„ décharné	„ bare.
„ fourchu	„ forked.
„ isolé	„ isolated
„ penché	„ leaning
Arbrisseau	Small tree
Arc	Arch.
Ardoisière, Ard⁶	Slate quarry.
Arrêt	Halt.
Asile	Asylum.
„ des } d' { aliénés	Lunatic asylum.
„ de charité	
„ des pauvres }	Asylum
„ de refuge	
Auberge, Aub⁶	Inn.
Aune	Alder-tree.
Bac	Ferry.
„ à traille	
Bains	Baths.
Place aux bains	Bathing place
Balise	Bouy, Beacon.
Banc de sable	Sand-bank.
„ vase	Mud-bank.
Baraque	Hut.
Barrage	Dam.
Barrière	Gate, Stile.
(Machine à) Bascule	Weigh-bridge.
Bassin	Dock, Pond.
„ d'échouage	Tidal dock

Bassin de radoub	Dry dock.
Bateau phare	Light ship.
Blanchisserie	Laundry.
B.M. (borne militaire)	Mile stone.
B⁴ (borne kilométrique)	
Boulonnerie Fab⁶ de boulons }	Bolt Factory.
Bouée	Bouy.
Brasserie, Brass⁶	Brewery.
Briqueterie, Briq⁶	Brickfield.
Brise-lames	Breakwater.
Bureau de poste	Post office.
„ de douane	Custom house.
Butte	Butt, Mound.
Cabane	Hut.
Cabaret, Cab⁶	Inn.
Câble sous-marin	Submarine cable.
Calvaire, Calv⁶	Calvary.
Canal de dessèchement	Drainage canal.
Canal d'irrigation	Irrigation canal.
Fab⁶ de caoutchouc	Rubber factory.
Carrière, Carr⁶	Quarry.
„ de gravier	Gravel pit.
Caserne	Barracks.
Champ de courses	Race course.
„ „ manoeuvres	Drill-ground.
„ „ tir	Rifle range.
Chantier	Skip yard.
Chantier de construction	Slip-way.
Chapelle, Ch⁶	Chapel.
Charbonnage	Colliery.
Château d'eau	Water tower
Chaussée	Causeway, Highway
Chemin de fer	Railway.
Cheminée, Ch⁶	Chimney.
Chêne	Oak tree.
Cimetière, Cim⁶	Cemetery.
Clocher	Belfry.
Clouterie	Nail factory.
Colombier	Dove-cot.

Coron	Workmen's dwellings
Cour des } marchan- { „ aux } dises	Goods yard.
Couvent	Convent.
Crassier	Slag heap.
Croix	Cross.
Darse	Inner dock.
Démoli · e	Destroyed.
Détroit · e, Dét⁶	
Déversoir	Weir.
Digue	Dyke, causeway.
Distillerie, Dist⁶	Distillery.
Douane	Custom house.
Bureau de douane	
Entrepôt de douane	Customs warehouse.
Dynamitière, Dynam⁶	Dynamite „ magazine.
Dynamiterie	Dynamite factory.
Écluse	
Échasette, Ech⁶	Sluice, Lock.
École	School.
Écurie	Stable.
Église	Church.
Émaillerie	Enamel works.
Embarcadère, Emb⁶	Landing-place.
Estaminet, Estam⁶	Inn.
Étang	Pond.
Fabrique, Fab⁶	Factory.
Fab⁶ de produits chimiques	Chemical works.
Fab⁶ de faïence	Pottery.
Faïencerie	
Ferme, F⁶	Farm.
Filature, Fil⁶	Spinning mill
Fonderie, Fond⁶	Foundry.
Fontaine, Font⁶	Spring, Fountain
Forêt	Forest.
Forme de radoub	Dry dock.
Forge	Smithy.
Fosse	Mine, Pit.
Fossé	Moat, Ditch.
Four	Kiln.
„ à chaux	Lime-kiln.

Four à coke	Coke oven.
Ganterie	Glove Factory.
Gare	Station.
Garenne	Warren.
Garnison	Garrison.
Gazomètre	Gasometer.
Glacerie Fab⁶ de glaces }	Mirror Factory.
Glacière	Ice factory.
Grue	Crane.
Gué	Ford.
Guérite à signaux	Sentry-box, Turret Signal-box (Ry.)
Halte	Halt.
Hangar	Shed, Hangar.
Hôpital	Hospital.
Hôtel-de-Ville	Town hall.
Houillère	Colliery.
Huilerie	Oil factory.
Imprimerie, Imp⁶	Printing works.
Jetée	Pier.
Laminerie	Rolling mills.
Ligne } de haute	High water mark.
Laisse } marée	Low „
„ de basse marée	
Maison Forestière M⁶⁶ F⁶⁶ }	Forester's house.
Malterie	Malt-house.
Marbrerie	Marble works.
Marais	Marsh.
Marais salant	Saltern, Salt marsh.
Marché	Market.
Mare	Pool.
Mât	Rick.
Minière	Mine.
Monastère	Monastery.
Moulin, M⁶	Mill.
„ à vapeur	Steam mill.
Mur	Wall.
„ crénelé	Loop-holed wall.

Nacelle	
Orme	
Orphelinat	
Oseraie	
Ouvrage	
Ouvrages hydrauliques	
Papeterie	
Parc	
„ aérostatique	
„ à charbon	
„ à pétrole	
Passage à niveau P.N.	
Passerelle, Pass⁶	
Pépinière	
Peuplier	
Phare	
Pilier, Pil⁶	
Plaine d'exercice	
Ponceau	
Pont	
„ levis	
Poste } de garde	
Station	
Poteau t⁶⁶	
Poterie	
Poudrière, Poud⁶	
Magasin à poudre	
Prise d'eau	
Puits	
„ artésien	
„ d'aérage	
„ ventilateur	
„ de sondage	
Quai	
„ aux bestiaux	
„ aux marchan- dises	
Raccordement	
Raffinerie	
„ de sucre	
Râperie	

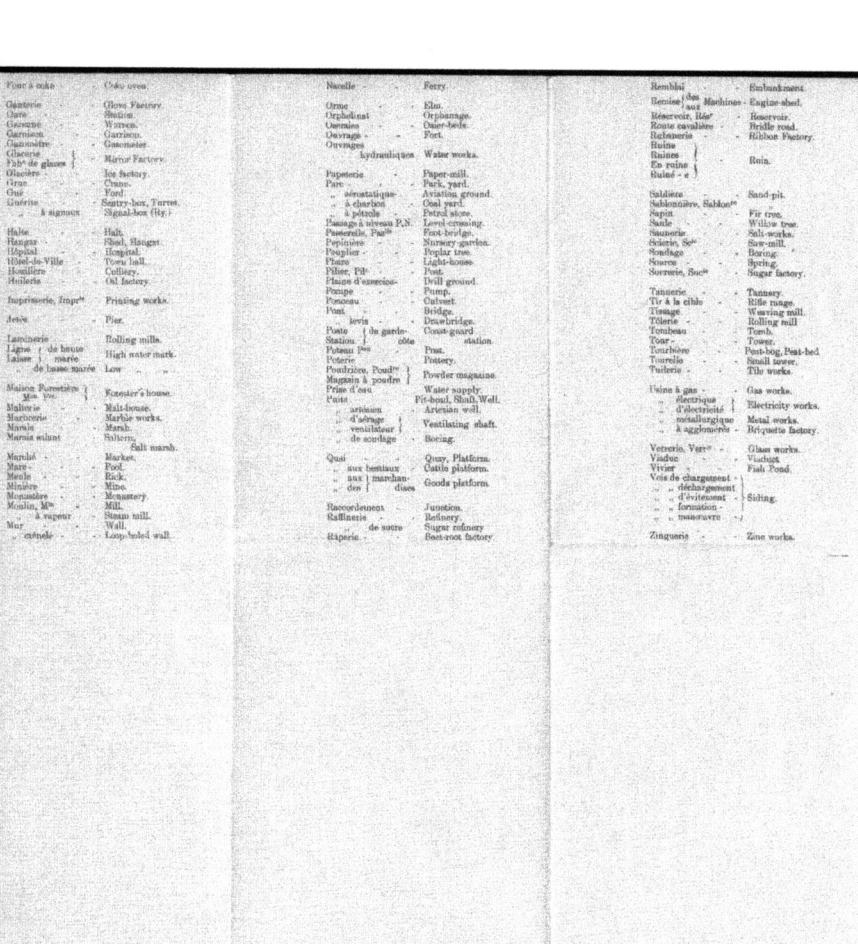

TRENCH MAP
FRANCE.
SHEET 51B S.W.
EDITION 4.A

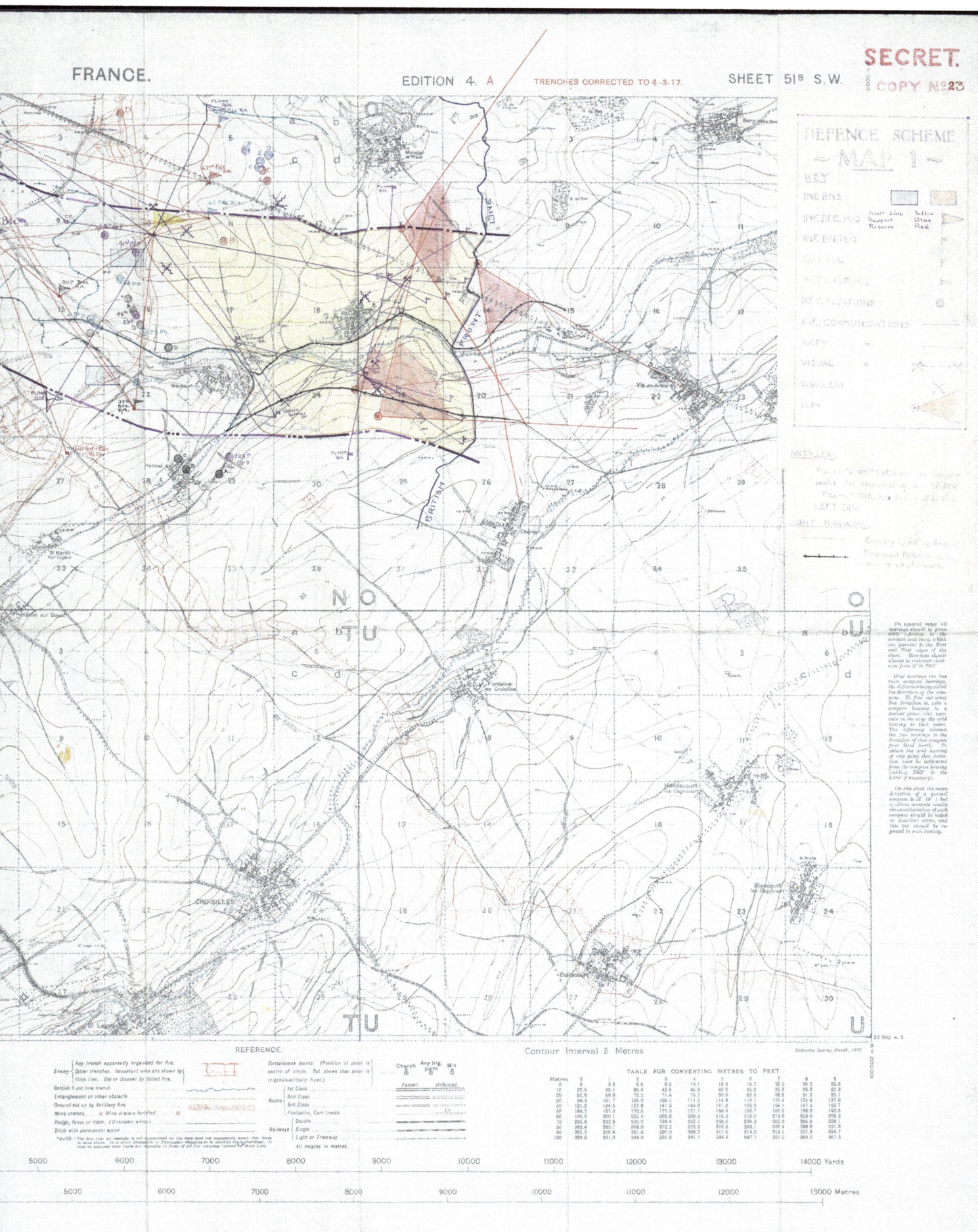

GLOSSARY.

Abbaye, Abb⁶	Abbey.
Abreuvoir, Ab⁶	Watering-place.
Abri de douaniers	Customs-shelter.
Aciérie	Steel works.
Aiguilles	Points (Ry.)
Allée	Alley, Narrow road.
Ancien - ne, Anc⁻ⁿ⁻ᵉ	Old.
Aqueduc	Aqueduct.
Arbre	Tree.
„ éventail	fan-shaped.
„ décharné	bare.
„ fourchu	forked.
„ isolé	isolated.
„ penché	leaning.
Arbrisseau	Small tree.
Arc	Arch.
Ardoisière, Ard⁶	Slate quarry.
Asile	Hlt.
„ d'aliénés	Asylum.
„ de charité	Lunatic asylum.
„ des pauvres	Asylum
„ de refuge	
Auberge, Aub⁶	Inn.
Aune	Alder-tree.
Bac	Ferry.
„ à traille	Ferry.
Bains	Baths.
Place aux bains	Bathing place.
Balise	Boom, Beacon.
Banc de sable	Sand-bank.
„ vase	Mud-bank.
Baraque	Hut.
Barrage	Dam.
Barrière	Gate, Stile.
(Machine à) Bascule	Weigh-bridge.
Bassin	Dock, Pond.
„ d'échouage	Tidal dock.

Bassin de radoub	Dry dock.
Bateau phare	Light-ship.
Blanchisserie	Laundry.
B.M. (borne milliaire)	Mile stone.
Bⁿ (borne kilométrique)	
Boulonnerie	Bolt Factory
Fab⁶ de boulons	
Bouée	Buoy.
Brasserie, Brass⁶	Brewery.
Briqueterie, Briq⁶	Brickfield.
Brise-lames	Breakwater.
Bureau de poste	Post office.
„ de douane	Custom house.
Butte	Butt, Mound.
Cabane	Hut.
Cabaret, Cab⁶	Inn.
Câble sous-marin	Submarine cable.
Calvaire, Cal⁶	Calvary.
Canal de dessèchement	Drainage canal.
Canal d'irrigation	Irrigation canal.
Fab⁶ de caoutchouc	Rubber factory.
Carrière, Carr⁶	Quarry.
„ de gravier	Gravel-pit.
Caserne	Barracks.
Champ de courses	Race-course.
„ manœuvres	Drill-ground.
„ tir	Rifle range.
Chantier	Building yard.
	Ship yard.
	Dock yard.
Chantier de construction	Slip-way.
Chapelle, Ch⁶	Chapel.
Charbonnage	Colliery.
Château d'eau	Water tower
Chaussée	Causeway.
	Highway.
Chemin de fer	Railway.
Cheminée, Ch⁶⁶	Chimney.
Chêne	Oak tree.
Cimetière, Cim⁶⁶	Cemetery.
Clocher	Belfry.
Clouterie	Nail factory
Colombier	Dove-cot.

Corons	Workmen's dwellings.
Cour des marchandises	Goods yard.
Couvent	Convent.
Crassier	Slag heap.
Croix	Cross.
Dune	
Darse	Inner dock.
Détruit - e, Dét⁶	Destroyed.
Déversoir	Weir.
Digue	Dyke, causeway.
Distillerie, Dist⁶	Distillery.
Douane	Custom-house.
Bureau de douane	
Entrepôt de douane	Custom warehouse.
Dynamitière, Dynam⁶⁶	Dynamite magazine.
Dynamiterie	Dynamite factory.
Écluse	Sluice, Lock.
Échauette, Éch⁶⁶	Sluice.
École	School.
Écurie	Stable.
Église	Church.
Émaillerie	Enamel works.
Embarcadère, Emb⁶⁶	Landing-place.
Estaminet, Estam⁶	Inn.
Étang	Pond.
Fabrique, Fab⁶	Factory.
Fab⁶ de produits chimiques	Chemical works.
Faïencerie	Pottery.
Ferme, F⁶⁶	Farm.
Filature, Fil⁶⁶	Spinning mill.
Fonderie, Fond⁶⁶	Foundry.
Fontaine, Font⁶⁶	Spring, fountain.
Forêt	Forest.
Forge de radoub	Dry dock.
Forge	Smithy.
Fosse	Mine, Pit.
Fossé	Moat, Ditch.
Four	Kiln.
„ à chaux	Lime-kiln.

Four à coke	Coke oven.
Ganterie	Glove Factory
Gare	Station.
Garenne	Warren.
Garnison	Garrison.
Gazomètre	Gasometer.
Glacerie	
Fab⁶ de glaces	Mirror Factory.
Glacière	Ice factory.
Grue	Crane.
Gué	Ford.
Guérite	Sentry-box, Turret.
„ à signaux	Signal-box (Ry.)
Halte	Halt.
Hangar	Shed, Hangar.
Hôpital	Hospital.
Hôtel-de-Ville	Town hall.
Houillère	Colliery.
Huilerie	Oil factory.
Imprimerie, Impr⁶⁶	Printing works.
Jetée	Pier.
Laminerie	Rolling mills.
Ligne de haute laisse marée	High water mark
„ de basse marée	Low „
Maison Forestière, M⁶⁶ F⁶⁶	Forester's house.
Malterie	Malt-house.
Marbrerie	Marble works.
Marais	Marsh.
Marais salant	Saltern.
	Salt marsh.
Marché	Market.
Mare	Pool.
Meule	Rick.
Minière	Mine.
Monastère	Monastery.
Moulin, M⁶⁶	Mill.
„ à vapeur	Steam mill.
Mur	Wall.
„ crénelé	Loop-holed wall.

Nacelle	Ferry.
Orme	Elm.
Orphelinat	Orphanage.
Ouvrage	Fort.
Ouvrages hydrauliques	Water works
Papeterie	Paper-mill.
Parc	Park, yard.
„ aéronautique	Aviation grⁿᵈ
„ à charbon	Coal yard.
„ à pétrole	Petrol store
Passage à niveau P.N	Level-crossing
Passerelle, Pass⁶⁶	Foot-bridge.
Pépinière	Nursery-grⁿᵈ
Peuplier	Poplar tree.
Phare	Light-house
Pilier, Pil⁶	Post.
Plaine d'exercice	Drill ground
Pompe	Pump.
Ponceau	Culvert.
Pont	Bridge.
„ levis	Drawbridge
Poste de garde	Coast-guard stⁿ
Station	
Poteau I⁶⁶⁶	Post.
Poterie	Pottery.
Poudrière, Poud⁶⁶	Powder mag
Magasin à poudre	
Prise d'eau	Water supp
Puits	Pit-head, Shaf
„ artésien	Artesian w
„ d'aérage ventilateur	Ventilating
„ de sondage	Boring.
Quai	Quay, Platf
„ aux bestiaux	Cattle platf
„ aux marchandises	Goods platf
Raccordement	Junction.
Raffinerie	Refinery.
„ de sucre	Sugar refin
Râperie	Beet-root fa

SECRET
TRENCH MAP

FRANCE.
SHEET 51B S.W.
EDITION 4.A

INDEX TO ADJOINING SHEETS

SCALE 1/20,000

	Coke oven.
	Glass Factory.
	Station.
	Warren.
	Garrison.
	Gasometer.
	Mirror Factory.
	Ice factory.
	Crane.
	Ford.
	Sentry-box, Turret.
	Signal-box (Ry.)
	Halt.
	Shed, Hangar.
	Hospital.
	Town hall.
	Colliery.
	Oil factory.
	Printing works.
	Pier.
	Rolling mills.
	High water mark.
	Low ...
	Forester's house.
	Malt-house.
	Marble works.
	Marsh.
	Saltern.
	Salt marsh.
	Market.
	Pool.
	Rick.
	Mine.
	Monastery.
	Mill.
	Steam mill.
	Wall.
	Loop-holed wall.

Nacelle	Ferry.
Orme	Elm.
Orphelinat	Orphanage.
Oseraie	Osier-beds.
Ouvrage	Fort.
Ouvrages hydrauliques	Water works.
Papeterie	Paper-mill.
Parc	Park, yard.
„ aérostatique	Aviation ground.
„ à charbon	Coal yard.
„ à pétrole	Petrol store.
Passage à niveau P.N.	Level-crossing.
Passerelle, Pss^lle	Foot-bridge.
Pépinière	Nursery-garden.
Peuplier	Poplar tree.
Phare	Light-house.
Pilier, Pil^r	Post.
Paine d'exercice	Drill ground.
Pompe	Pump.
Ponceau	Culvert.
Pont	Bridge.
„ levis	Drawbridge.
Poste de garde-côte	Coast-guard station.
Poteau I^que	Post.
Poterie	Pottery.
Poudrière, Poud^re	Powder magazine.
Magasin à poudre	
Prise d'eau	Water supply.
Puits	Pit-head, Shaft, Well.
„ artésien	Artesian well.
„ d'aérage	
„ ventilateur	Ventilating shaft.
„ de soudage	Boring.
Quai	Quay, Platform.
„ aux bestiaux	Cattle platform.
„ aux marchandises	Goods platform.
Raccordement	Junction.
Raffinerie	Refinery.
„ de sucre	Sugar refinery.
Râperie	Beet-root factory.

Remblai	Embankment.
Remise des Machines aux	Engine-shed.
Réservoir, Rér^r	Reservoir.
Route cavalière	Bridle road.
Rubanerie	Ribbon Factory.
Ruine	
Ruines	Ruin.
En ruine	
Ruiné	
Sablière	Sand-pit.
Sablonnière, Sablon^re	
Sapin	Fir tree.
Saule	Willow tree.
Saunerie	Salt-works.
Scierie, Sc^ie	Saw-mill.
Sondage	Boring.
Source	Spring.
Sucrerie, Suc^ie	Sugar factory.
Tannerie	Tannery.
Tir à la cible	Rifle range.
Tissage	Weaving mill.
Tôlerie	Rolling mill.
Tombeau	Tomb.
Tour	Tower.
Tourbière	Peat-bog, Peat-bed.
Torrelle	Small tower.
Tuilerie	Tile works.
Usine à gaz	Gas works.
„ électrique d'électricité	Electricity works.
„ métallurgique	Metal works.
„ à agglomérée	Briquette factory.
Verrerie, Verr^ie	Glass works.
Viaduc	Viaduct.
Vivier	Fish Pond.
Voie de chargement	
„ déchargement	
„ d'évitement	Siding.
„ formation	
„ manœuvre	
Zinguerie	Zinc works.

www.ingramcontent.com/pod-product-compliance
Lightning Source LLC
Chambersburg PA
CBHW081412160426
43193CB00013B/2161